TEACHING IDEA DEVELOPMENT

TEACHING IDEA DEVELOPMENT

A Standards-Based Critical-Thinking Approach to Writing

Sharon Crawford Hatton
Pam Leneave Ladd

CORWIN PRESS, INC.
A Sage Publications Company
Thousand Oaks, California

For information:

Corwin Press, Inc.
A Sage Publications Company
2455 Teller Road
Thousand Oaks, California 91320
E-mail: order@corwinpress.com

Sage Publications Ltd.
6 Bonhill Street
London EC2A 4PU
United Kingdom

Sage Publications India Pvt. Ltd.
M-32 Market
Greater Kailash I
New Delhi 110 048 India

Printed in the United States of America

Library of Congress Cataloging-in-Publication Data

Hatton, Sharon Crawford.
   Teaching idea development: A standards-based critical-thinking approach to writing / by Sharon Crawford Hatton and Pam Leneave Ladd.
      p. cm.
   Includes bibliographical references.
   ISBN 0-7619-7758-9 (c : alk. paper) — ISBN 0-7619-7759-7 (p : alk. Paper)
   1. Critical thinking—Study and teaching—United States. 2. English language—Composition and exercises—Study and teaching—United States. 3. English language—Study and teaching—Standards—United States.
4. Interdisciplinary approach in education—United States.   I. Ladd, Pam
Leneave. II. Title.
 LB1590.3 .H39 2001
 808'.042'071—dc21   2001000624

This book is printed on acid-free paper.

02 03 04 05 06 07 7 6 5 4 3 2 1

Acquiring Editor: Rachel Livsey
Corwin Editorial Assistant: Phyllis Cappello
Production Editor: Diane S. Foster
Editorial Assistant: Cindy Bear
Typesetter/Designer: Denyse Dunn
Cover Designer: Michelle Lee

Contents

Preface

Few university teaching programs, or early teaching experiences, adequately prepare teachers for instructing their students in writing for authentic purposes and audiences, in a variety of real-world forms. Yet to meet the communications standards for a 21st-century education, both teachers and students must be able to think more critically and write with ideas fully developed in authentic forms for readers. National reading standards require that students be able to analyze a variety of authentic texts. Nationwide, in public and private schools, colleges and universities, educators and students are facing the challenge of how to think critically about ideas in reading and for writing.

Educators search for practices that lead students to success. Our experience as education consultants and teachers ourselves led us to begin an analysis of the problems writers reveal. We then began to examine the critical link between thinking skills and strategies necessary for writers to successfully develop ideas. Although certainly not a new concept, the idea development approach we offer here attempts to establish a more successful connection to the manner in which writers actually produce text.

For students to internalize the abstract notion of idea development, the abstraction must become concrete. Yet once idea development is recognized as a concrete skill or strategy, the danger exists that some instructors will teach it in isolation, as is often the case with grammar and mechanics. It is *not* our intent that students apply skills in this isolated manner. Research and test scores support the premise that such isolated instruction is an exercise in futility. Writers learn to write through instruction with application to their own writing.

The answer to students' writing difficulties lies in teaching idea development as an authentic thinking process rather than as an assignment focusing on one or two strategies taught in isolation. Although for the purpose of this particular text the format reflects a sequential order of skill acquisition, the concept should not be taught in isolation, but rather in the context of classroom reading, writing, and thinking instruction when applicable to student developmental learning. The reading-writing-thinking sequences described in the following pages will assist teachers as they instruct students to internalize the strategies successful writers use when developing ideas.

Essential to the approach espoused in this book is our philosophy that writing instruction must be viewed as more than an academic exercise; it is an opportunity for students to learn a communication skill extending beyond the English curriculum.

WHAT YOU WILL FIND IN THIS BOOK

For students to acquire the skills necessary for successful communication of ideas, teachers must create multiple learning opportunities in the classroom. The format of Chapters 3 through 10 is uniform, for easy reference of the specific idea development strategy. Section topics include the following:

- Definitions
- Examples
- Characteristics
- Supporting and expanding idea development
- Understanding the concept as support for ideas
- Understanding applications in writing
- Applications to writing
- Assessing the strategy
- Examples of the strategy to be used as classroom models

Chapter 1 shares with teachers the importance of teaching the components of idea development and describes a classroom approach to instruction. Through the approach prescribed, students analyze complete texts to determine the reasoning behind a writer's purposeful development of ideas and self-assess their own work to determine idea development strengths and needs.

Chapter 2 emphasizes the importance of adequately preparing students before they place pen to paper. Strategies are introduced in this chapter to assist student writers as they prepare to design and complete writing tasks. Teachers will learn the importance of diagnosing causes of weakness in student writing and designing instruction to improve students' writing skills. Specific problems with possible solutions are offered.

Chapter 3 addresses the importance of purposeful details for informative or technical writing, which must appeal to readers on an intellectual rather than an emotional level. Activities in this chapter identify, define, and provide instruction for teaching purposeful details that expand readers' understanding. Using this process, students become more selective about the details used to develop ideas.

In **Chapter 4,** activities for teaching description include applications for both practical and subjective description to clarify and convey information accurately, with regard to the purpose and audience identified. The activities lead students to become critically discriminating when selecting the type and specificity of description to be employed in their writing. A variety of descriptive applications are presented.

Chapter 5 approaches the concept of comparison and contrast as an idea development strategy rather than as a form of writing. Activities promote an understanding of the concept of comparison-and-contrast analysis and an understanding of the strategy's application in writing. The instruction described will assist students in thinking through and developing comparison-and-contrast support beyond a superficial reference. Students will critically assess writing situations for the application of this support in their writing.

Chapter 6 addresses the importance of cause-and-effect reasoning, which is woven through all genres of writing and which often serves as the basis for other types of support. Activities provide opportunities for students to understand the concept, its application in the writing of others, and its usefulness in their own writing. Teacher-directed activities lead student writers through a thinking-writing process designed to eliminate cause-and-effect confusion.

Chapter 7, on dialogue as an idea development strategy, contains activities that enable student writers to determine the most appropriate purposeful dialogue to communicate an idea to a reader. Teacher-directed instruction focuses on preparing students to become autonomous assessors of effective and ineffective dialogue.

Chapter 8's mini-lessons address appropriate use and development of anecdotes. Teachers facilitate as students learn to recognize anecdotes from text and consider their effectiveness as an idea development strategy. From this analysis, activities lead students to craft anecdotes, eliminating unsupported generalities, oversimplification, circular thinking, unsubstantiated opinions, and repetition.

In **Chapter 9,** instructional activities address the variety of literary purposes for the vignette. Teaching strategies focus on the language decisions a writer uses to develop an image quickly and powerfully for a reader.

Chapter 10 leads student writers through several analysis activities to establish a knowledge base for future application. Activities include teaching students the process of taking a large idea or situation and breaking it into its component parts. Mini-lessons help students understand relationships between component parts and the whole. Other activities lead students to consider an audience as they produce text that allows for reflective connections by the reader.

WHO SHOULD READ THIS BOOK AND WHY

In this book, we examine idea development and its relationship to critical thinking in a manner that promotes understanding by even the most inexperienced instructor. It is our hope that the writing development techniques in this book will provide novice and veteran intermediate, middle, and high school teachers a touchstone text they can access, reference, or use for refining their own writing instruction. These instructional ideas were designed for use with students in both whole class and individual instruction settings.

Additionally, teachers of content areas other than English and language arts face particular needs with regard to reading, writing, and thinking. The careful analysis of critical-thinking skills and their connection to writing offered in this text will assist teachers of all content areas as they provide effective, integrated instruction for their students.

College and university teacher-preparation programs are under fire in many states, especially those where educational reform efforts are aligned with national standards. Our book will assist preservice teachers as they acquire the knowledge base necessary to be effective and successful first-year teachers. These education students will discover instructional sequences and mini-lessons that allow for manageable writing instruction.

Individual writers, too, may apply the sequences and instruction contained herein to enhance their writing abilities and build their confidence as writers.

As curriculum specialists who are committed to implementing a standards-based curriculum in our own schools and districts for the teaching of writing, we offer this specialized approach to improve writing scores. Our own experience suggests that other curriculum specialists will find this text equally beneficial.

ACKNOWLEDGMENTS

For the challenges they presented and their support, we wish to thank

> Kentucky teachers and their students, as through their growth, we, too, have grown
>
> The Kentucky Department of Education for the opportunity to focus our own learning and acquire the skills and knowledge necessary to assist teachers
>
> Former and present Kentucky Writing Program consultants: our friends, our thinking partners, our colleagues who share the vision and see the "big picture"
>
> Our families, who have believed in us throughout

SHARON CRAWFORD HATTON
PAM LENEAVE LADD

The contributions of the following reviewers are also gratefully acknowledged:

Karen Evans
Vice President
Interactive Media and Distance Learning Product Development
SkyLight Professional Development (a Pearson Education Company)
Arlington Heights, Illinois

Judith Brush Griffith, PhD
Assistant Professor of English
Director of Secondary English Education
Wartburg College
Waverly, Iowa

Tom Leverett
Lecturer
CESL, Southern Illinois University at Carbondale
Carbondale, Illinois

Sarah Edwards
Teacher Educator
University of Arizona
Tucson, Arizona

Maria Elena Reyes
Assistant Professor
School of Education
University of Alaska Fairbanks
Fairbanks, Alaska

About the Authors

Sharon Crawford Hatton is currently the Curriculum and Assessment Coordinator at Western Elementary School in Georgetown, Kentucky. Previously, she was one of eight Kentucky Writing Program consultants with the Kentucky Department of Education for 7 years. Her classroom experience includes teaching at the high school level for 9 years and at the middle school level for 4 years.

As a writing consultant, she worked with 185 schools to develop successful writing programs and curriculum. During this time, she conducted numerous workshops, both locally and nationally, while providing ongoing technical assistance to teachers in Kentucky. While with the Kentucky Department of Education, she coauthored *Sharpen Your Child's Writing Skills*, wrote articles for teacher publications, and developed training materials that continue to be the basis for teacher professional development and training.

Recently, she has taught classes at Eastern Kentucky University; assisted AEL, Inc., with research for developing effective schoolwide writing programs; and worked with the Jefferson County Public School District in Louisville, Kentucky, as an external evaluator of the Edna McConnell Clark Foundation Grant. In her spare time, she enjoys reading and golf.

Pam Leneave Ladd is an education consultant and 30-year educator. After 21 years in primary and high school classrooms, she served for 8 years as a K-12 Kentucky Writing Program consultant, through the beginning years of reforming the state's education system. Her practical classroom and consultation experiences with writing portfolios, performance-based assessment, and related research have defined her career in writing education. She has led thousands of workshops and provided ongoing services to schools since her experiences with National Writing Projects, beginning in the 1980s.

Coauthor of *Sharpen Your Child's Writing Skills* and various articles and writing training materials, she is presently the in-school writing consultant for students and teachers at Cooper-Whiteside Elementary School in Paducah, Kentucky, through a federal CSRD grant program. In addition, through her educational consulting firm, Writing Connections, Inc., she leads professional development workshops and provides other reading-writing-related services.

A former recipient of Ashland Oil's Teacher Achievement Award, she has recently taught graduate classes in teaching writing in schools at Murray State University. She assisted AEL, Inc., with research for developing effective schoolwide writing programs. A presenter at many national conferences, she also serves on the Kentucky Professional Standards Board Continuing Education portfolio coaching and scoring cadre.

The mother of daughters Ashlea and Alison, she is also a "spare-time" antiques aficionado (with her husband, Roy), house renovator, and book lover.

Part I

Implementing Idea Development in the Classroom

Promoting Effective Writing

WHAT IS IDEA DEVELOPMENT?

Idea development is the substance of a piece of writing. Without it, the writing is superficial and insignificant—full of generalities, unsubstantiated claims, and empty verbiage—a waste of a reader's time.

A need or desire for communication precedes every significant piece of writing. The writer has a reason to share ideas and information with a reader who needs or desires further understanding. Once a writer has established a purpose and an audience, he or she then determines the ideas necessary to communicate the purpose to that particular audience. These two factors, purpose and audience, control all further decisions.

When the writer chooses to share the same ideas with a different audience, the support for the ideas will likely change. Before developing the ideas, a writer must first analyze the intended audience. The audience's educational or technical background; knowledge of the subject; and preference in format, style, and organization must be considered. After this analysis, the writer selects specific information and strategies appropriate to develop the ideas for this new audience.

Effective writers understand and consciously employ the subtleties of writing. As readers, they appreciate a skillful writer's careful development of ideas to deepen a reader's understanding. Most students, however, are not yet this skilled. Therefore teachers should guide students in acquiring necessary writing and reading skills through purposeful instruction and opportunities for authentic communication. Individual inquiry and critical-thinking skills, integrated in daily instruction, will assist students in becoming independent thinkers and writers.

To strengthen idea development in their writing, students often must think on paper. They must also explore the many facets of content as learners. Their thinking and experiences must be validated by others. Teachers can facilitate student thinking and learning by implementing supportive classroom practices such as the following:

- Teach specific critical-thinking and idea development strategies through direct instruction and repeated reinforcement within the total curriculum
- Connect learning experiences to students' life experiences and interests
- Institute use of a writer's notebook—a cache for student reflection and a springboard for future writing—in which each student investigates and makes personal connections to learning and learning processes
- Respect the variety of authentic roles students bring to their writing
- Link reading and writing instruction to analyze strategies writers employ and make connections to students' own writing
- Analyze effective and ineffective writing form and genre models to expand students' understanding of idea development strategies
- Provide adequate time, instruction, and response to students during prewriting as they make decisions about purpose, audience, ideas, form, and organization
- Promote students' transfer of newly learned skills and strategies to previously written pieces in working folders to aid in the revision process
- Conference during all developmental stages of a piece of writing

Through such focused facilitation, teachers create an environment where writing is an outgrowth of thinking and learning.

Effective idea development showcases the writer's critical-thinking skills —deep thinking, reasoning, and reflection about purpose and ideas. This thinking is made tangible through the specifics provided to help a reader understand the ideas being communicated. The significance of ideas and independent thinking revealed through their development makes the written communication successful or unsuccessful. As students become skilled thinkers, the quality of ideas in their writing will improve.

TEACHING STUDENTS TO UNDERSTAND IDEA DEVELOPMENT

The purpose of the activities in this text is to help students comprehend the concept of idea development and its importance to written communication. Before students can benefit from instruction in specific idea development, they must understand that it is the development of ideas that makes writing "good." The instructional steps suggested here will lead students to recognize idea development as a significant factor in effective writing, analyze writing for the reasoning behind a writer's purposeful development of ideas, and assess their own work to determine idea development strengths and needs.

Once students have a better understanding of the role idea development plays in effective writing, they are ready to learn specific idea development strategies for use in authentic writing tasks (see Table 1.1). They will then be prepared to make informed decisions about which specific strategies will deepen their readers' understanding. The mini-lessons in this section establish the context of complete written texts, a necessary precursor to the chapters on specific strategies to follow.

Analyzing Whole Texts for Idea Development

1. Read aloud several pieces of writing or portions of several pieces of writing. Include examples of expressive (personal narrative, personal essay, memoir), literary (short story, poem, play), and transactive (article, editorial, letter, or other form) writing unless you are teaching one of these types and addressing idea development as a part of that instruction. In this case, limit your examples to one type.

2. Lead students in a discussion of their reactions to the writing. List responses on an overhead transparency or chart. Look for patterns in their responses and connect them to specific idea development strategies. Are they referencing practical or subjective descriptive passages (introductions, conclusions, passages leading to the most significant part of a narrative or story, the most significant part itself), vignettes, dialogue passages, anecdotal passages, cause-and-effect examples, compare-and-contrast examples? (See Table 1.1 for a list of some specific idea development strategies.) Ask questions such as the following:

- Which of the pieces did you find to be the most interesting or enjoyable? Why?
- Which part do you remember best? Why do you think it is the most memorable?
- Which part did you like best? Why?
- In which part did you feel most involved or engaged as a reader or listener? Why?
- In which parts did the writer appear to provide information that caused you to reflect, question, or think beyond the text? Why do you think this was so?

3. Ask students to bring to class pieces of writing they found interesting or enjoyable. In learning logs, students will reflect on why they have selected the piece. Using the list of strategies in Table 1.1, students can attempt to identify the strategies the writer has chosen to include. This should give you some idea of their current knowledge base and assist you in planning needed instruction. Included at the end of Chapter 1 are personal expressive and transactive samples for use with instructional activities. Although these are elementary samples, they may be used for the purpose of analysis at any grade level. You may wish to substitute others to support instruction in your classroom.

TABLE 1.1   Some Specific Idea Development Strategies: What Writers Use to Help Readers Understand

Vignettes	Analyzing Audience Point-of-View
Anecdotes	pros and cons
Cause and Effect	reactions
Compare and Contrast	personal connections
Descriptions	opinions
practical/technical	questioning
subjective	Purposeful Details
word choice	schematics
sensory details	flowcharts
strong nouns and verbs	diagrams
allusions	examples
similes	pictures
metaphors	illustrations
personification	charts/tables
onomatopoeia	graphs
alliteration	lists
assonance	quotes
consonance	statistics
hyperbole	facts
Dialogue	directions/instructions
Analogies	definitions
Analysis/Reflection	references
personal connections	Organizational/Audience Awareness
opinions	headlines
reactions	titles
reasons	subheadings
questions	offsets/insets
flashback	fonts
foreshadowing	bold print
imaginings	captions
emotions	transitions
thoughts	visual images

To determine the characteristics of effective and ineffective writing, ask students to read two pieces of writing of the same form and talk about the differences they see. Which of the two is the more effective piece? Why? Record the reasons as students mention them aloud. Make connections to the following standards-based assessment criteria: purpose and audience awareness, idea development and support, organization, sentences, language, correctness or surface features.

Analyzing Narratives

1. Using the following questions, read and analyze "My Experience on the Adventure Express" (the reading sample on page 12). The questions provided here may be used for any type of writing being analyzed. The answers in parentheses are particular to "My Experience on the Adventure Express."

- What is the writer's focused purpose for writing? (To share with readers the way he felt when he rode the Adventure Express, and his reaction to the experience.)
- Where in the piece do you, the reader, know what that focused purpose is? ("Once it started moving, things changed quickly." "I was very frightened." "I don't hardly see why anyone with any sense would want to ride on a ride like the Adventure Express.")
- How does the writer give the reader a context for the information? (The title provides information for the reader. The writer makes reference to the ride and how fast it goes in the opening paragraph.) How does the writer draw the reader into the piece? (The first sentence states the significance of the event for the writer. Also, the description of the ride and the language used to explain the action help to draw the reader into the experience.)
- How does the title establish a context and suggest the purpose? (The reader knows that the ride was an "experience," then discovers why the "experience" was memorable.)
- What main idea(s) does the writer choose to develop? (How his anticipation of the ride began, his fear during the ride, the physical description of the ride, and his feelings after the ride.)
- Are the ideas organized to assist the reader chronologically (time order); spatially (visual order); with order of importance (least to most or most to least); with foreshadowing (outcome clues provided early in the text); with flashback (interruption to recall an earlier event); or with other techniques specific to the piece being analyzed? (The writer used chronological order.)

What visual images or events occur in the chronological sequence? (Analysis may take the form of sequential drawings of the narrative.)

2. Provide other narratives for students to analyze similarly.

Analyzing Informational Writing

1. Using the following questions, read and analyze "How to Do the Electro-magnet" (the reading sample on page 13).

- What is the writer's focused purpose for writing? (To provide instructions for making an electromagnet)
- Where in the piece do you, the reader, know what that focused purpose is? (Opening paragraph)
- How does the writer give the reader a context for the information? (Asks a question of the reader and provides a purpose for needing an electromagnet)
- How does the title establish a context and suggest the purpose? (It is an allusion to a once-current dance craze and suggests that the result will be the successful creation of an electromagnet.)
- What main idea(s) does the writer choose to develop? (The materials needed, the procedure to follow, and the results of successfully following the instructions)
- How are the ideas organized to assist the reader? (Sequentially)

2. Provide other content-related informational reading for students to analyze similarly. This type of task extends specific content learning and reading skills as well as providing the basis for later writing.

3. Demonstrate the creation of an idea web or cluster from the purpose, main ideas, and support of a completed text, referred to as a "backmap." (A backmap will resemble a plan a writer might have prepared prior to drafting.) An analysis activity of this type allows students to make a reading/writing connection to the piece while examining the relationships of the ideas/support and the construction/organization.

4. Have students read "Three-Leaf Danger," on page 14. Use the backmap, also included at the end of the chapter (Figure 1.1), to discuss the purpose, audience, and primary and secondary ideas. Discuss how backmapping may be used to analyze a piece of writing. Emphasize its usefulness as a critical-reading strategy.

5. After students read "Three-Leaf Danger," refer to the questions below for discussion of the specific support strategies the writer used.

- What types of support do you notice in the introduction and conclusion? (Expected responses are subjective description, cause and effect, and comparison. At this point, students may respond using other terms.)
- Which part of the article contains the most subjective description, and why do you suppose the author included it there? (The introduction, to engage the reader)
- What strategy is used to disclose the purpose? (Comparison)

- What clue about purpose is provided by the title? (The reader may know that poison ivy has three leaves. The word *danger* implies that the plant may cause harm.)
- What strategy is used to introduce the primary ideas? (The writer uses questions to establish transition and identification of the primary ideas: "Why are plants a problem?" and "What can you do about poison ivy?")
- What factual information is provided in the quote? (Avoid three-leafed plants.)
- In the fifth paragraph, how are facts used to support cause-and-effect statements? (The facts explain how to alleviate the situation created in the cause-and-effect statements.)

Analyzing Fiction

1. Have students read *Wilfrid Gordon McDonald Partridge* by Mem Fox (1995). Use a backmap (or other graphic organizer) to discuss the purpose, audience, and primary and secondary ideas. Discuss how backmapping may be used to analyze a piece of writing. Emphasize its usefulness as a critical-reading strategy.

2. Direct students to reread the first seven pages from *Wilfrid Gordon McDonald Partridge.* Refer to the specific idea development strategies in Table 1.1 to discuss support strategies the writer used.

- What types of support do you notice in the introduction? (Practical and subjective description)
- What is the purpose of practical description in the introduction? (Introduces characters and setting and communicates protagonist's relationships to other characters)
- What strategy is used to disclose the purpose or introduce the problem? (Dialogue)
- What strategy is used to introduce the primary ideas? (Questioning)

Now reread the final pages.

- Which development strategies are used; how do they support the primary ideas? (Dialogue, sensory details, figurative language, practical description, snapshots, anecdotes, and emotions)

Comparison and Contrast Support Strategies for Different Forms

1. Ask students to look again at their answers to the questions on "Three-Leaf Danger" and *Wilfrid Gordon and McDonald Partridge.* Ask such questions as the following:

- How are the strategies in the two different?
- How are they alike?
- What conclusions may be drawn about appropriate support for informative writing?
- What conclusions may be drawn about appropriate support for literary writing?
- What differences may be noted regarding the introductions and conclusions?

2. Follow the same process with "My Experience on the Adventure Express" and *Wilfrid Gordon McDonald Partridge* or another text of your (or your students') choice.

Creating Graphic Representations of Text

1. Have students reread "My Experience on the Adventure Express." Use a prewriting visual or story map for students to create, with a partner, a graphic or visual representation of "My Experience on the Adventure Express," showing the purpose of the piece, primary and secondary ideas, and order of its parts.

Then students should use the list of idea development strategies in Table 1.1 to identify support strategies used in "My Experience on the Adventure Express" by highlighting the text and labeling the supports used. You may wish to do this as a whole class activity.

2. Using the highlighted copy of "My Experience on the Adventure Express," ask students to answer the following questions:

- What types of support do you notice in the introduction?
- What is the purpose of using these types of support in the introduction?
- What strategy is used to disclose the purpose?
- What strategies are used to introduce or develop the primary ideas?
- What strategies are used to develop the secondary ideas?

3. Students then reread "Do the Electromagnet." Individually or with a partner, ask students to create their own graphic or visual organizer for "Do the Electromagnet" showing the purpose, audience, and primary and secondary ideas. Remind students there are a variety of ways to graphically organize the analysis of a piece of writing (i.e., clusters, webs, backmaps, lists, outlines).

Analyzing for Specific Support Strategies

1. Have students use the list in Table 1.1 to identify support strategies used in "Do the Electromagnet" by highlighting the text. You may wish to do this as a whole class activity.

2. Using the highlighted copy of "Do the Electromagnet," ask students to answer the following questions:

- What types of support do you notice in the introduction?
- What is the purpose of using these types of support in the introduction?
- What strategy is used to disclose the purpose?
- What strategies are used to introduce or develop the primary ideas?
- What strategies are used to develop the secondary ideas?

3. Ask students to look again at their highlighted copies of "My Experience on the Adventure Express" and "Do the Electromagnet."

- How are the strategies in the two different?
- How are they alike?
- What conclusions may be drawn about appropriate support for informative writing?
- What conclusions may be drawn about appropriate support for personal expressive writing?
- What differences may be noted regarding the introductions and conclusions?

INTRODUCTIONS AND CONCLUSIONS

The introduction and conclusion are key to the success of any piece of writing. Although students may be able to effectively analyze introductions and conclusions, they still have difficulty creating their own. A strong introduction provides the reader with insight into the purpose and establishes the need for specific primary ideas and their support. An effective conclusion logically evolves from the ideas developed, provides the reader with a sense of closure, and reinforces the purpose. Student writers/readers must understand the connections between the introduction, the ideas and support, and the conclusion of a well-constructed piece of writing. A classroom analysis of introductions and conclusions may use the same process as that outlined for other parts of the text.

ASSESSING THE ACTIVITIES

The activities in this chapter are for the purpose of teaching students to identify writers' support strategies in order to implement these standards-based strategies in their own writing. Therefore formal assessment of the activities is unnecessary. As students complete the activities, the students themselves, their peers, and the teacher should provide informal assessment. This necessary feedback will ensure that students have internalized the concept and skills taught. Teachers may wish to extend the activities by analyzing classroom reading or reevaluating previous student writing.

EXAMPLES TO BE USED AS CLASSROOM MODELS

The following samples are included for instructional use with the mini-lessons in this chapter. Elementary writing is often useful with writers of any age or experience level to illustrate concepts and strategies.

MY EXPERIENCE ON THE ADVENTURE EXPRESS

I will never forget the day I went to Kings Island and rode the Adventure Express. It was my first trip ever to the amusement park. I hadn't missed any days of school and all of the students who came every day for a whole year got a free trip to Kings Island as a reward.

I was really excited about the trip. Everyone who had been before had told me all about the different rides, but my Sunday school teacher had told me that the Adventure Express was the best. She said it really went fast!

When we got to the park, I rode the Bumper Cars first. I thought I'd start out small and work my way up. After four or five rides, I felt like I was ready for the Adventure Express.

The Adventure Express looked a lot like a roller coaster. I had to walk through a building to get on it. It didn't look like it was going to be a bit scary, and at first, it wasn't. Once it stared moving, things changed quickly.

I was very frightened. The ride took me up steep hills. When the cars came back down, it felt like the bottom had dropped out and my car wasn't even on the track anymore.

I held on tight and hunkered down in the seat as the cars went around sharp curves. It jerked me and swung me from one side of the car to the other. I was screaming as loud as I could.

The ride shot through long, dark tunnels on what looked like a broken track. There were snakes and ghosts on the walls. I could hear the ghosts screaming and moaning. The tracks were creaking like they were going to break. Steam shot up around the cars and drops of water fell back on me. My heart was beating so fast I could almost hear it.

I couldn't wait for the ride to be over. When it finally stopped, I was in shock. When I got off that thing, I could barely even talk. I was so shook up I wasn't able to stand up. I felt sick at my stomach too and had to go to the bathroom.

I don't hardly see why anyone with any sense would want to ride on a ride like the Adventure Express. It jarred me around and made me think I was going to be thrown out and go flying through the trees. I thought sure I was going to have a stroke or a heart attack before it was over.

After that experience, I do know this much. If I ever go to Kings Island again, I am only going to ride the Bumper Cars and other easy rides. I am done with all of those fast rides forever!

(4th-Grade Student)

NOTE: Used with permission of the Kentucky Department of Education, Frankfort, Kentucky 40601.

HOW TO DO THE ELECTROMAGNET

Ever wonder how you can pick up paper clips without using your hands? Now you can by making an electromagnet. If you don't know how, then follow these simple instructions.

1. First you need to gather these items: 2 D batteries, 2 battery holders, 4 clips, 2 wires—7 inches long, and 1 big nail. Once you have all of these items, you're set to make an electromagnet.

2. Put the batteries in the battery holders. Make sure you have one battery facing north and one facing south.

3. Put a clip in each end of both holders facing out.

4. When you're done doing that, get a wire and slip it into one of the clips on the first holder. Slip the other end of the wire into a clip on the second holder. Now the holders are connected by one wire. Connect your other wire to the clip on the opposite end of the second holder.

5. Wrap the loose end of the wire leading from the second holder about 10 coils around the nail. Leave some wire hanging off the nail.

6. Slip the loose end of the second wire into the open clip on the first holder.

7. Scatter the paper clips on a flat surface. You can use the top or bottom of the nail to pick them up.

8. For more power, increase the coils by 10 on the nail. Wrap tightly, then you'll be able to pick up more paper clips.

When you're done making this easy electromagnet, you'll have lots of fun picking up paper clips.

(4th-Grade Student)

NOTE: Used with permission of the Kentucky Department of Education, Frankfort, Kentucky 40601.

THREE-LEAF DANGER

If you've ever had it, you know the incredible itching. The large red bumps or blisters. Yes, poison ivy or its relatives, poison oak and poison sumac, can turn a fun summer outing into an itchy nightmare.

Why are these plants such a problem? For one thing, nearly three out of four people are allergic to them. What's more, the plants grow just about everywhere in North America. The allergen in these plants is contained in an oil found on almost any part of the plant. So it's not just the leaves that are dangerous.

This oil rubs off easily on clothes or skin when you brush against it. And pets that roam where poison ivy grows can bring it back to you on their coat. In fact, even the smoke from burning poison ivy can cause the rash on some people.

What can you do about a pesky rash maker like poison ivy? Learn to know the plant. The old saying "Leaves of three, leave them be" can help you remember what it looks like.

If you do get poison ivy on your skin, wash those areas with soap as soon as possible. The soap breaks down the oil and reduces the allergic reaction. Doing this within 10 minutes can stop rashes or blisters before they start. If the poison ivy is on your clothes, don't touch them until you get home. Take them off without touching the parts that were in the ivy.

If you've already broken out, calamine lotion or hot water with baking soda or corn starch can help reduce the itching. If the poison ivy gets bad or you have a history of bad poison ivy, see your doctor to get other medications. Of course, the best way to avoid this nasty rash is to know what the plants look like—and stay away!

("Three-Leaf Danger," 1994, p. 3)

SOURCE: *Current Health*® 1 Magazine, © Copyright 1994 by Weekly Reader Corp. All rights reserved.

CHAPTER SUMMARY

Idea development is the most critical factor in effective writing. Successful idea development showcases a writer's conscious employment of the subtleties of writing and rewards the reader with engagement and understanding. In a standards-based program, teachers provide students with learning opportunities to recognize the inherent thinking in a variety of reading materials. As students become proficient at analyzing written text for the idea development employed by writers, they begin to reflect these strategies in their own writing.

Figure 1.1: Backmap for "Three-Leaf Danger"

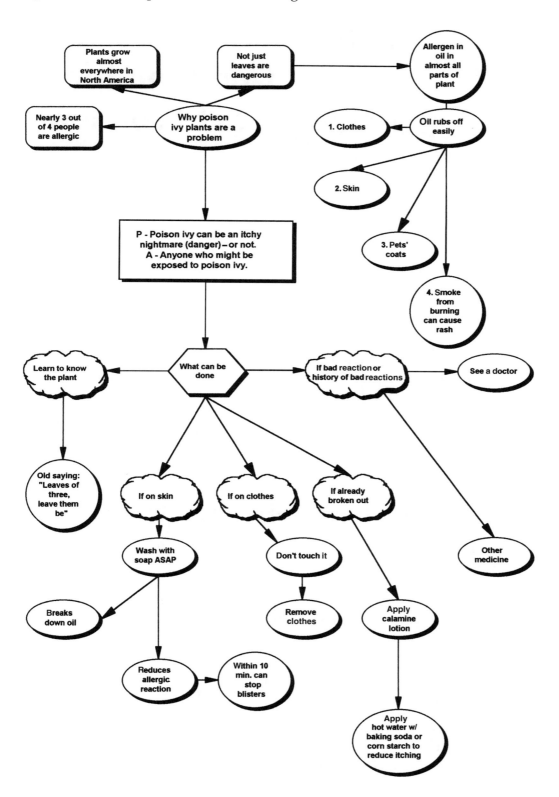

2 ◆ Identifying and Solving Common Idea Development Problems

"More idea development needed."
"You are writing well about nothing."
"This piece of writing lacks idea development."
"Why is this important?"
"How does this support your purpose?"

Do these common teacher comments sound familiar? What prevents our students from making the all-important thinking-writing connection? Could the reason be that these writers have not yet learned the importance of preliminary thinking and planning to meet the needs of readers?

Most students think about a writing task or topic only briefly and superficially before they begin to draft. Even when the topic is one they have selected and know well, the resulting writing is often ineffective. For students to improve their written products, we must provide opportunities for them to acquire effective and efficient thinking-process habits.

By definition, a habit is not innate; it must be taught, learned, and reinforced. Students follow our lead. If we make an assignment one day and expect the draft the following day, we are suggesting that the task requires minimal thinking preparation. Instead, from their earliest classroom writing experiences, students should be taught to focus their writing prior to drafting. Through this careful, structured thought, many causes for ineffective writing can be eliminated. A proactive teacher diagnoses the causes of weakness in student writing and designs instruction to improve students' writing skills. The results of such specific attention help students develop habits that will carry over into their future thinking and writing situations.

AVOIDING COMMON PROBLEMS IN IDEA DEVELOPMENT

Once the causes are diagnosed, the following suggestions for direct instruction may be useful in teaching effective thinking and writing habits.

Purpose and Audience Communication Considerations

Unsuccessful writing quite often is a direct result of the writer's disconnection from a clear purpose and audience. Frequently this is the case with "classroom" writing, written for the teacher merely for a grade.

Problem

Topic-Driven Rather Than Purpose-Driven Writing. When writing is focused on a topic rather than a purpose, the communication that results will be broad and overgeneralized. Primary ideas will often be unrecognizable, with little or no relationship between the ideas presented.

Possible Solutions

To solve the problem of topic-driven writing, writers should do the following:

1. Prior to drafting, students should generate possible purposes from a larger topic. They might ask themselves, "What interests me about this topic? Is anything unusual or different about this topic? What is the least understood aspect of my topic? What would a particular person or group of people find useful to know and why?"

2. Once they have selected a purpose for writing from their own roles or concerns, they must think through their roles and concerns regarding the purpose. A possible useful question is, "Why is this purpose important to me?"

3. To generate possible ideas necessary to communicate the purpose, an appropriate question for student writers to ask is, "What primary ideas could I possibly include for my selected audience and purpose?" This process encourages students to select the ideas that will best develop the purpose and that are meaningful to the writer. A further useful question is, "Which primary ideas are necessary for understanding the purpose?"

4. To consider the role the selected audience will play in how the ideas will be developed, the student writer will ask, "What does the audience need or want to know about this topic? What does the audience already know about this topic? What should I include to help the audience understand?"

Problem

Too Many Primary Ideas. Writing that contains too many primary ideas will produce (a) superficial coverage of ideas; (b) lack of strong, supporting secondary ideas; (c) overlapping of ideas and their support; and (d) different ideas developed with similar support.

Possible Solutions

Prior to drafting, writers should take the following steps:

1. Generate possible ideas necessary to communicate the purpose, and group those ideas by like characteristics to determine the primary ideas. This may be accomplished by asking, "Which ideas have something in common?"

2. Eliminate ideas that may have little or no relationship to the purpose by questioning, "How do my ideas relate to the purpose?"

3. From those remaining, select the most significant ideas to effectively develop the purpose. A useful question is, "Why are these ideas are necessary to communicate my purpose?" Students should be encouraged to keep selection to a minimum. Successful writers generally develop very few primary ideas.

Problem

Too Few or Poorly Developed Secondary Ideas. Generality expression (trite statements); poorly substantiated primary ideas; and failure to meet audience expectations, needs, or connections are all problems that result from poorly developed or too few secondary ideas.

Possible Solutions

Prior to drafting, to prevent problems with secondary ideas, writers should follow the following process:

1. Consider the role the audience will play in how the ideas will be developed. Questions to assist with the role of the audience are, "What examples could I give that would help my audience understand? What, if any, visuals would help my reader and what reasons could I supply?"

2. Plan to develop each primary idea with secondary ideas that (a) are meaningful to the audience, (b) meet the needs of the audience, (c) provide necessary

information and thinking connections for the audience, (d) allow the audience to think critically about the purpose, and (e) reflect the writer's experience.

3. Generate possible secondary ideas necessary to develop each primary idea. A graphic organizer is useful for this planning.

4. Eliminate ideas that may have little or no relationship to the primary idea by asking a question such as, "How do the secondary ideas relate to the primary idea?"

5. Select the most significant secondary ideas from those remaining that will most effectively develop the primary idea by determining, "What makes these the most significant?"

6. Plan to develop each secondary idea with specific support that (a) is meaningful to the audience, (b) meets the needs of the audience, (c) provides necessary information and thinking connections for the audience, (d) allows the audience to think critically about the purpose, and (e) reflects the writer's experience.

7. Determine the specific support (idea development strategies) that will best bring the reader to a complete understanding of the ideas by asking, "Why did I select these specific strategies?" or "Why are they more effective than others?"

Problem

Inclusion of Inappropriate or Ineffective Support. Problems with idea development resulting from inappropriate or ineffective support are (a) lapses due to failure to sustain focus on a purpose, and (b) confusion for the reader from unrelated or irrelevant information.

Possible Solutions

Prior to drafting, writers should do the following:

1. Eliminate primary ideas, secondary ideas, and support that may have little or no relationship to the purpose by asking "How do these ideas relate to each other and the purpose?"

2. Select the most significant ideas and support that will effectively develop the primary idea by asking "What makes these significant?"

3. Develop ideas with specific support that

- Are meaningful to the audience
- Meet the needs of the audience
- Provide necessary information and thinking connections for the audience
- Allow the audience to think critically about the purpose

♦ Reflect the writer's experience

4. Determine the specific support (idea development strategies) and organize it to provide the reader with a complete understanding of the ideas by asking "Why did I select these specific strategies? Why are they more effective than others? Which information does the reader need first? How do these ideas relate to each other?"

Mode/Form Considerations

Problem

Inclusion of Support Neither Pertinent nor Effective for the Chosen Form. Writing that includes support that is neither pertinent nor effective for the chosen form will cause confusion for the reader due to (a) unmet expectations, or (b) failure to fulfill characteristics required by the form.

Possible Solutions

Prior to drafting, writers should do the following:

1. Read and analyze examples of the chosen form of writing and ask "Where is the purpose stated? How is the reader drawn in? What kinds of support are used? Where does the writing connect with the reader?"

2. Understand the characteristics of the chosen form by asking "What makes the writing a story, a memo, a memoir, a speech, an editorial, or another form of writing?"

3. Select a form of writing appropriate to the purpose and audience by asking "What form of writing does my purpose dictate?"

4. Generate primary and secondary ideas and support that are appropriate to the form and best meet the needs of the audience

Problem

Presentation of Ideas Is Neither Appropriate nor Effective for the Chosen Form. Problems with idea development will include confusion for the reader due to (a) unmet expectations, (b) failure to fulfill characteristics required by the form, or (c) failure to adequately communicate with the audience. The ideas and support may also (d) fail to maintain the context provided by the introduction, or (e) fail to lead the reader to the stated conclusion.

Possible Solutions

Prior to drafting, writers should do the following:

1. Determine support strategies appropriate to the chosen form that best meet the needs of the audience.

2. Consider strategic placement of ideas and support within the constraints of the form to best meet the needs of the audience.

3. Read examples of the chosen form and analyze introductions and conclusions for connections to the ideas developed by asking "How is the reader drawn into the writing? How does the writer provide closure for the reader? How are the primary ideas connected to the introduction and conclusion?"

4. Plan to develop ideas through support that will sustain the context of the planned introduction. Ask, "When considering my primary and secondary ideas, which will carry out what I have planned in the introduction?"

5. Consider a conclusion that will provide closure for the ideas to be developed and maintain the context of the planned introduction. Ask, "What, if anything, do I want my reader to do after reading? Have I left my reader with unanswered questions? How is my purpose reflected in my conclusion? In what way have I connected the conclusion to the introduction?"

Many student writing problems are a result of limited or ineffective prewriting. As students develop thinking and writing habits, their writing will improve. Since more time has been devoted to actively planning the writing and structuring the thinking, less time will be required for extensive revision.

INEFFECTIVE SUPPORT STRATEGIES

Successful writing consists of well-crafted primary ideas that develop and communicate a purpose to an audience. Inexperienced writers sometimes rely on primary ideas alone to convey the message. In other cases, inexperienced writers attempt to develop primary ideas with support that fails to clarify their thinking and expand the reader's understanding. Although the writing may appear to be elaborated, the reader gains no significant insight because the writer's reasoning is illogical or unclear.

Such imprecision in writing is often the result of limited prewriting or unproductive revision. Adequate thinking and planning time prior to drafting is essential to successful idea development. Later, when ideas are revised, writers should use the opportunity to deepen the reader's analysis and understanding of the ideas, rather than to simply add more.

Inadequate thinking and reasoning are often revealed when writers depend on ineffective support strategies to develop ideas. Writing must reflect students' abilities to think critically and correctly apply that thinking in their writing. Although thinking is abstract, it becomes concrete through writing. Successful writing instruction provides opportunities for students to discover and employ strategies to make their thinking concrete and manageable.

PROBLEMS IN THINKING

Oversimplification

To reduce the use of ineffective support strategies, writers must first recognize them in their own writing. Eliminating ineffective strategies alone does not guarantee sound writing. However, the following will assist teachers as they instruct students to identify and eliminate unsatisfactory support for the development of ideas. Examples resemble those in student writing.

Oversimplification results from drawing conclusions that assume more than the facts support.

Example

I believe that recycling is the answer to problems facing humans across the globe. (The issue of global problems is oversimplified by proposing that the problems can be solved merely by recycling.) *Problems such as global warming, toxic dumping, and animal and plant life habitat destruction. The problems I just named are just scratching the surface.* (The phrase "just scratching the surface" without support oversimplifies the significance of these global problems.)

Teaching Techniques

Provide instructional opportunities for students to do the following:

- Analyze passages that contain oversimplified support, in order to question the implications of the statements
- Revise oversimplified samples to make them more meaningful to the reader while not altering the writer's intended idea
- Examine their writer's notebooks or collections of their own writing to identify oversimplifications
- Revise identified oversimplifications for clarity

Provide other mini-lesson opportunities to discuss and revise oversimplified statements to help students establish a positive thinking and writing process.

Unsupported Generalities

Unsupported generalities employ excessively broad statements, draw conclusions with little or no support, or use broad statements in lieu of support. Concluding generality statements are appropriate when they follow logically from the support provided.

Example

I think that all humans should join together and help save the earth. No matter what gender, religious background, race, age, or color, humans are all in danger. (When removed from the piece, the proceeding statement is not specific to the writer's identified topic of recycling.) *We should all work toward a common goal: curing the disease that is spreading like a pox over the planet, the disease of pollution.* (This general call to action fails to explain how this goal can be accomplished.)

Teaching Techniques

Provide instructional opportunities for students to do the following:

♦ Analyze passages that contain unsupported generalities, in order to determine questions posed by the unsupported generality
♦ Revise unsupported generality samples by providing various answers to the questions they evoke
♦ Embed the answers in the piece, providing more meaning for the reader while not altering the writer's intended idea
♦ Examine writer's notebooks or collections of their own writing to identify unsupported generalities
♦ Revise identified generalities for clarity

Provide other mini-lessons to discuss and revise generality statements as often as necessary to assist students in establishing a revision habit.

Circular Thinking

Circular thinking repeats the same assertion without actually ever providing support for it.

Example

We do have a problem with deadly drugs in our community. Parents and citizens need to be informed of the problem. The problem is only going to become worse and worse, and that is why parents and citizens should take heed of the warning and quit ignoring the problem. It will not just disappear on its own. (The third sentence merely restates the first two sentences without providing any new information or reflection on previously presented information.)

Teaching Techniques

Provide instructional opportunities for students to

- Recognize circular thinking through mapping the redundancy of primary ideas or support in a piece of writing
- Combine like support to reduce redundancy
- Examine the revision, looking for ways to provide stronger support for the remaining ideas
- Examine writer's notebooks or collections of their own writing to identify circular thinking
- Revise identified circular thinking for clarity

Provide other mini-lesson opportunities to discuss and revise circular thinking passages when it is a critical problem in students' writing.

Repetition of Ideas

Presenting the same or a similar idea as if it were a different idea or developing the same idea in a variety of ways are two forms of repetition.

Using a Different Context or Different Phrasing

Example

Recycling is a habit not to be enforced but to be embraced with open arms. Once people see the advantages of recycling, they will join the bandwagon. I think all humans should join together and help save the earth. (Each sentence repeats the idea of everyone recycling.)

Teaching Techniques

Provide instructional opportunities for students to do the following:

- Differentiate between repetition of ideas and repetition of support for different ideas
- Differentiate between purposeful repetition that enhances meaning and unintentional repetition that detracts from meaning
- Recognize repetition by mapping primary ideas or support
- Identify the primary ideas and eliminate repetition of these ideas or identify the repetition of support for different primary ideas
- Analyze the primary ideas and determine the most effective support strategies to develop the ideas
- Analyze primary ideas developed through repetitious support
- Determine effective and varied support strategies to develop ideas
- Examine writer's notebooks or collections of their own writing to identify repetition of ideas or support
- Revise repetition of ideas or support for clarity

Provide other mini-lessons to discuss and revise repetitive passages whenever this problem surfaces as a pattern in student writing.

Using Different Word Choices

Example

As I stepped out into the frigid morning air, puffs of white steam escaped my mouth while I called out to my friends at the icy bus stop. When I plopped down on the vinyl bus seat, I could feel the chill all the way through my jeans. (Each sentence expresses the idea of cold.)

Teaching Techniques

Provide instructional opportunities for students to do the following:

- Differentiate between purposeful repetition that enhances meaning and unintentional repetition that detracts from understanding
- Recognize repetition of word denotation and connotation through mapping the support in a piece of writing
- Determine from their mapping the most appropriate word choices to convey the meaning of the passage
- Examine writer's notebooks or collections of their own writing to identify repetition of words and phrases
- Revise identified repetition for clarity

Provide other mini-lessons to discuss and revise repetitive words or phrases evident in student writing.

Unsubstantiated Opinions

Unsubstantiated opinions are arguments based solely on the writer's opinion.

Example

The situation at our school has gotten worse. There are too many problems to ignore. We must take immediate action. (No attempt was made to explain how the situation has become worse, what "too many" problems are, or what actions are needed. The reader has no knowledge of the writer as an authority, nor does the writer credit an authority to substantiate the opinions given.)

Teaching Techniques

Provide instructional opportunities for students to do the following:

- Examine writer's notebooks or collections of their own writing to identify unsubstantiated statements
- Revise identified unsubstantiated statements for clarity

Provide mini-lesson opportunities to discuss, revise, and supply pertinent support for unsubstantiated statements.

Testimonials From Nonauthorities

Testimonials from nonauthorities include self-testimonials and crediting information to an uninformed source.

Example

I believe global warming, toxic dumping, and animal and plant life habitat destruction are the three most critical problems facing humans across the globe. (The reader is asked to accept the beliefs of the writer, a nonauthority.) *Some people say part of the state of California will fall into the Pacific Ocean when California has its next earthquake.* (The writer fails to credit an authority to substantiate the opinion.)

Teaching Techniques

Provide instructional opportunities for students to do the following

♦   Analyze sources to determine level of credibility
♦   Examine writer's notebooks or collections of their own writing to identify the following: nonauthority statements, self-testimonials, the words *believe, think, feel*
♦   Revise identified passages

Provide mini-lesson opportunities to discuss and consider possible authorities for statements.

Appeals to Ignorance

An appeal to ignorance is claiming that a belief must be true since no one has disproved it or must be false since it has not been proven.

Example

Show me one study that proves that I'll live longer if I drive slowly. (Implies that without positive proof the claim must be false.) *I put much faith in horoscopes because mine is seldom wrong.* (Claims that a belief must be true since no one can disprove it.)

Teaching Techniques
Provide instructional opportunities for students to do the following:

♦   Analyze appeals to ignorance, examining them for words such as *if* and *because* to determine the thinking represented

- ◆ Examine writer's notebooks or collections of their own writing to identify appeals to ignorance statements
- ◆ Revise identified appeals to ignorance statements for clarity

Provide mini-lesson opportunities to discuss, revise, and clarify statements such as the appeal to ignorance examples above.

False "Either-Or"

False "either-or" means presenting two ideas as cause-and-effect based only on speculation or assumption. (One idea does not necessarily follow from the other.) False either-or most often appears in the argument of someone who is not expecting a reply.

Example

If you don't buy your new car here, you'll pay too much (implies that other car dealerships overcharge customers).

Teaching Techniques
Provide instructional opportunities for students to do the following:

- ◆ Examine false either-or statements to identify the relationship of the parts, to determine if logic warrants each relationship, and, if not, to phrase a more logical relationship
- ◆ Examine writer's notebooks or collections of their own writing to identify false either-or statements
- ◆ Revise identified false either-or statements for clarity

Provide mini-lesson opportunities to discuss, clarify, revise statements.

Half-Truths

Half-truths are based only partly on fact or use one fact to support an opinion.

Example

More young people than ever before are cheating on tests, so we can't trust students at our school to be honest (fails to establish a credible cause-and-effect relationship).

Teaching Techniques
Provide instructional opportunities for students to do the following:

- ◆ Examine half-truth statements to identify the "conclusion" drawn, determine if evidence is provided to warrant that conclusion, and if not, phrase a more valid conclusion

- Examine writer's notebooks or collections of their own writing to identify half-truths
- Revise identified half-truths for clarity

Reinforce with mini-lesson opportunities as needed.

PROBLEMS IN LANGUAGE

Examples

- *Slanted Language. My neighbor's young son is a menace to society.* (The writer adds a persuasive bias through choice of words with negative connotations.)
- *Subjective Adjectives. She was wearing a beautiful dress. This apple tastes awful.* (The writer fails to supply definitive words, such as sequined or sour, or a more descriptive phrase or passage to enhance the reader's understanding.)
- *General Nouns and Pronouns. Bring me the paper. Give me that.* (The writer fails to use a specific word, such as *newspaper* or *stationary*, resulting in ambiguity for the reader or listener.)
- *Weak Verbs. The principal went down the hall.* (The writer fails to select verbs, such as *charged, strode, stomped*, that allow the reader to picture the action.)
- *State-of-Being Verbs. The group of singers was at the auditorium.* (The writer fails to select verbs such as *arrived,* or *performed* to describe action for the reader.)

Teaching Techniques

Provide instructional opportunities for students to do the following:

- Use the examples above and others you have noted from student writing to identify language problems and craft solutions
- Locate ineffective and effective examples of language use in newspapers and magazines
- Examine writer's notebooks or collections of their own writing to identify language problems
- Revise language problems for clarity and effectiveness

Provide mini-lessons to generate and record in writer's notebooks possible substitutions for ineffective examples of the language problem(s) being addressed.

ASSESSING THE ACTIVITIES

The activities in this chapter teach students to identify ineffective support strategies and to place more emphasis on the prewriting stage of their writing. Informal assessment of activities includes (a) assessing prewriting before students begin to draft and (b) focusing on ineffective support strategies evident in student drafts.

This feedback will ensure that prior to drafting, students have internalized concepts and skills and are able to make draft-enhancing revisions. Teachers may extend the activities by analyzing classroom reading or reevaluating previous student writing.

CHAPTER SUMMARY

All too often, teachers hand out an assignment and then await the stellar finished product. This chapter emphasizes the importance of adequately preparing students before they place pen to paper. The strategies introduced in this chapter will assist student writers as they prepare to design and complete writing tasks. As students "think through assignments," as suggested here, they will be better prepared to produce clear, concise, thought-provoking written communication.

Eliminating common problems in idea development as well as ineffective support strategies is crucial to the production of student writing that reflects standards-based instruction. Through teaching students to examine texts for ideas and their development, teachers will promote lifelong reading, thinking, and writing skills.

Part II

Strategies for Teaching Idea Development

Purposeful Details

3

Most students and their teachers are familiar with the purposeful details and support found in literary reading and writing. They are often less knowledgeable about the purposeful details and support found in personal expressive, reflective, and informative or technical reading and writing. Yet most adult communication is likely to be in these forms. Purposeful details add to the purpose of the writing and are carefully selected to best communicate an idea to the intended audience. Sometimes purposeful details used by writers are in the form of visuals, which provide readers with specific information or a particular perspective on information.

Although purposeful details are inherent to all types of writing, certain of these details are used only in technical or informative writing, where the audience's needs are much more specific. For example, an architect prepares a proposal and accompanying presentation, including diagrams and flowcharts, for a corporation board. The team manager for telephone company technicians communicates in a memo to a supervisor the cost analysis of a proposed improvement plan. A medical patient writes a business letter to an insurance company providing documentation for a claim. All three of these scenarios require the writer to have knowledge of purposeful details development, an area of writing instruction often overlooked in schools.

To assist students in acquiring skills to communicate to a variety of audiences, for a variety of purposes, through appropriate forms, teachers must provide opportunities for students to read and analyze many types of texts. The analysis of these articles, personal essays, proposals, technical reports, and other published forms will provide students with a knowledge base for their writing while reinforcing content learning.

Informative or technical writing, unlike most expressive and literary writing, presents ideas that appeal to readers on an intellectual rather than an emotional level. If the writer's purpose is to convince a reader through reasoned research or to inform for a specific purpose, the ideas the writer selects are often developed through objective and factual details. If the writer's intent is to engage the reader on a more personal reflective level, details might be more subjective. In either case, clear communication depends on the writer's ability to intentionally select and include details that expand the reader's understanding.

Students who understand the uses of purposeful details support in different types of writing have little difficulty communicating information to a reader. They are knowledgeable about the specific types of details most appropriate for their purpose and audience. They are more likely to use correct terminology, appropriate examples, credible sources, accurate quotes, and useful data representations as they develop ideas.

TEACHING STUDENTS TO USE PURPOSEFUL DETAILS

Purposeful details are individual or minute parts of a whole. They provide itemized or specified treatment of particulars toward a focused purpose.

Characteristics of Purposeful Details

- Support the writer's purpose
- Meet specific needs of the reader
- Clarify the ideas being developed
- Add needed information
- Provide *whats*, *whys*, and *hows* for the reader
- Enrich and enliven the writing

Supporting and Expanding Idea Development

Purposeful details support main ideas and expand thinking by the following;

- Considering readers' backgrounds, experiences, and frames of reference
- Selecting only the details most important and relevant to the point being made
- Elaborating to ensure writing is reader-based, not writer-based
- Reducing the chances for misunderstanding by providing the reader with a clear interpretation of what is being developed
- Showing action, description, and specifics, rather than telling about them
- Ensuring that details blend to produce a cohesive, smoothly flowing whole

---

UNDERSTANDING THE USE OF PURPOSEFUL DETAILS

The purpose of the learning activities in this chapter is to teach idea development strategies for students to apply independently. When students have a clear understanding of the uses of purposeful details as support for idea development, the teacher, during written or face-to-face conferencing, may suggest these devices to add depth. Students should record writing-to-learn activities from the following mini-lessons in a learning log or writer's notebook for later reference.

Facts

Definition
Facts are true and accurate information that support, substantiate, or expand an idea.

Tips for Using Facts

- Select facts for which proof can be obtained.
- Document facts either in the text or with some type of accepted means of documentation.

- Elaborate facts, when necessary, with analysis or reflection.
- Use facts to provide support for opinions or generalizations.

Example

DNA can be detected from a microscopic drop of blood, a fallen hair, or a drop of saliva. No two individuals have the same DNA makeup. Use of DNA identification in criminology is one of the most significant recent advances in that field.

Statistics

Definition

Statistics are numerical facts that support, substantiate, or expand ideas.

Tips for Using Statistics

- Make sure statistics are correct.
- Select statistics that can be substantiated.
- Provide limited interpretation of statistics.
- Use statistics sparingly and selectively.

Example

In the past several years, many advances have been made in the field of breast cancer research. If an effective cure for this disease is to be found, many more millions of dollars must be available for the continuation of this research. Every year over *46,000* women die of breast cancer; approximately *3/4* of these cases occur in women *50* years of age or older. In fact, *one out of every eight* women in America has the chance of contracting this form of cancer. *Eighty percent* of these women have no breast cancer history. Because of the magnitude of the problem, it is likely, through family or friends, that every person will in some way be affected by this disease. As you make your pledge to the American Cancer Society, know that your donation may save the life of someone you know.

Examples

Definition

Examples are details that answer the reader's question, "What do you mean by that statement?" They provide illustration of ideas—specific cases, objects, or instances—appropriate to the purpose and the audience.

Tips for Using Examples

- Choose examples that support the general statement or idea.

- Choose examples with the audience in mind.
- Do not veer off into an interesting side issue.
- Determine the number of examples needed.
- Use several examples when dealing with trends.
- Determine the type of example necessary; that is, the simple mention of an example, lists of similar examples in logical sequence, or an extended example in narrative form.

Example

The life of a student is very difficult in today's society. *In addition to schoolwork and activities, students are responsible for many other tasks. Many students have after-school jobs that require them to juggle their time and energies. Other students have responsibilities at home—caring for younger siblings; helping with household chores; or, in some cases, running the household for a working parent.* Just a few days ago, I overheard one of my students talking to a friend about all the things he did after school. *First, he stopped at the elementary school to pick up one of his sisters and drop her off at the baby-sitter's house. Fifteen minutes later, he was punching in at work. After a seven-hour shift at McDonald's, he still had to revise a scientific article for his physics class and read and analyze an editorial for Current Issues 201. Before he could even think about going to bed, he unloaded the dishwasher and prepared his younger sisters' lunches for the following day. Finally, at 2:15 a.m. he was able to fall in bed, totally exhausted.*

Lists

Definition

Lists are a way of presenting information that allow the reader to see specifics at a glance and allow key ideas to stand out.

Tips for Creating and Using Lists

- Use parallel structure.
- Use single words, phrases, or short sentences.
- Provide adequate transitions before and after lists.
- Use bullets when rank or sequence is not important.
- Do not overuse lists.

Example

In today's society, few people are able to exercise to the extent they would like or need to exercise. More and more people are looking for ways to make exercising a part of their daily routine. When you consider the benefits of regular exercise, the need is obvious.

> ### Advantages of Feeling Better
>
> ♦ Gives you more energy
> ♦ Helps you cope with stress
> ♦ Increases your resistance to fatigue
> ♦ Helps you to relax and feel less tense

Illustrations

Definition

Illustrations are a means of presenting facts and ideas to a reader in a way that words alone could never make clear. The *Handbook of Technical Writing* directs,

> Illustrations should never be used as ornaments; however, they should always be functional, working parts of the writing. Use an illustration only when it makes a direct contribution to the reader's understanding of the subject. When creating illustrations, consider your objective and your reader. (Shelton, 1994, p. 137)

Tips for Creating and Using Illustrations

♦ Make the significance of each illustration clear in the text.
♦ Include in the text a transition or direct reference to each illustration.
♦ Position as close as possible to, but not before, the referencing text.
♦ Present only one type of information in each illustration.
♦ Keep information as brief and simple as possible.
♦ Label or caption each illustration accurately.
♦ Keep terminology consistent.
♦ Make lettering for headings or titles horizontal, if possible.
♦ Allow white space around and within illustration for easy viewing.
♦ Include a key that identifies all symbols, when necessary.
♦ Specify proportions or include scale of relative distances, when appropriate.

Examples

All types of illustrations can be located in mathematics, social studies, and science texts; popular print media, such as magazines and journals; and technical publications. Although most students have been exposed to illustrations such as these in their content area classes, many may have forgotten the proper design and use of each, and most students have had little instruction in how they are used to enhance idea development. Teachers who are in the habit of collaborating with colleagues may already be considering the sources mentioned above as possibilities for teaching or teaming. Such collaboration offers opportunities to analyze content area reading for the writing strategies inherent to different disciplines.

Graphs As Illustrations

Definition

Graphs are the visual representation of numerical data that show trends, movement, distributions, and cycles. Graphs take the form of line graphs, circle graphs, and bar graphs.

Tips for Creating and Using Line Graphs

- Label each graph numerically as Figure 1 (or Fig. 1), Figure 2, and so on.
- Include a horizontal scale, which should indicate independent (changing) variables, any increases from left to right, and the variables if the value is not time.
- Include a vertical scale, which should indicate dependent (unchanging) variables, any increases from top to bottom, and the type of variable if the value is not time.
- Represent data in multiple lines, if necessary.
- Use line graphs to show relationships between two sets of numbers (e.g., trends, movements, relationships, and cycles), usually over time.

Tips for Creating and Using Circle or Pie Graphs

- Begin the largest segment in the "12 o'clock" position.
- Moving clockwise, continue with next largest segment.
- Place items that individually would occupy small segments together in a final segment labeled "Other" or "Miscellaneous."
- Place the label and the percentage or amount on or near each segment.
- Use circle or pie graphs for showing simultaneous comparison of parts to one another and comparison of one part to the whole.

Tips for Creating and Using Bar Graphs

- Include one or more horizontal or vertical bars of equal width.
- Put a scale along the length to represent amounts or quantities.
- Subdivide a bar to represent multiple data or crosshatch, color, or shade to indicate different divisions.
- Use a bargraph to show immediate comparisons of amounts or quantities.

Tables As Illustrations

Definition

A table represents data in a concise form by providing numerous facts and is more accurate than a graph.

Tips for Creating and Using Tables

- ◆ Use tables to present large amounts of data concisely.
- ◆ Number each table, unless it has a descriptive title.
- ◆ Label each column accurately and concisely.
- ◆ Use standard symbols and abbreviations.
- ◆ Use decimals instead of fractions.
- ◆ Include all factors or information that affect the data.
- ◆ Use ample spacing and rule lines (straight lines).
- ◆ Repeat column headings if the table is divided for continuation.

Organizational Charts As Illustrations

Definition

Organizational charts show how various components of an organization are related to one another.

Tips for Creating and Using Organizational Charts

- ◆ Use organizational charts to give readers an overview of an organization or show lines of authority within an organization.
- ◆ Place the title of each component in a separate box.
- ◆ Arrange blocks on the same level to suggest the same level of authority.
- ◆ Connect boxes by lines to indicate arrangement; use heavier lines to show chain of authority; use broken lines to show coordination, liaison, or consultation.

Flowcharts As Illustrations

Definition

Flowcharts are diagrams of a process that involves stages, with the sequence of the stages shown from beginning to end.

Tips for Creating and Using Flowcharts

- ◆ Use flowcharts to show flow or sequence of related actions quickly and easily.
- ◆ Label clearly and concisely.
- ◆ Assign the chart a figure number, if necessary.
- ◆ Use blocks, triangles, circles, or labels to represent the steps.
- ◆ Use arrowhead lines to show direction the sequence moves.
- ◆ Include a key for symbols, if necessary.
- ◆ Place each flowchart as near as possible to the text containing a reference to it.

Diagrams or Schematic Diagrams As Illustrations

Definition

A diagram can be a plan, sketch, or outline consisting primarily of lines and symbols, rather than a physical likeness, that demonstrates or explains a process, object, or area and clarifies the relationship existing among the parts of a whole.

Tips for Creating and Using Diagrams or Schematic Diagrams

♦ Use diagrams to show the shape and location of items and their function and operation.
♦ Use diagrams to show the operation of the subject.
♦ Keep information as brief and simple as possible.
♦ Label or caption carefully.

Directions or Instructions

Definition

Directions or instructions are used to explain how to perform a specific task and should be based on clear thinking and careful planning to enable a reader to carry out the task successfully.

Tips for Creating and Using Directions or Instructions

♦ Understand thoroughly the task being described.
♦ Keep in mind the reader's level of knowledge and experience.
♦ Include special tools or materials necessary to complete the task.
♦ List all essential equipment at the beginning.
♦ Write instructions as written commands, in the imperative.
♦ Phrase instructions concisely, but make sure they are easily understood and contain all essential information.
♦ Divide instructions into short, simple, sequential steps.
♦ Do not sacrifice clarity for conciseness.
♦ Alert readers to steps that require precise timing or measurement.

Example

Writers should be clear about their task prior to beginning a transactive draft. The first thing to do is read and examine models of the genre or form of writing to be attempted. After understanding the qualities of this type of writing, identify the purpose for your own writing. Next determine who has a need or desire for this information and analyze this audience. The final series of steps in prewriting requires writers to generate the ideas necessary to communicate the purpose to the identified audience and select or locate the supporting information needed to develop the ideas. The degree of attention given to the writing task prior to drafting significantly reduces the amount of time spent during revision.

Definitions

Definition

To define is to clarify the meaning of a word, phrase, or term.

Tips for Creating and Using Definitions

- Define either formally (using classification) or informally (by providing a familiar word or phrase as a synonym), depending on the purpose and on the reader.
- Focus on what the term is, rather than on what it is not.
- Avoid circular definitions, restating the term to be defined.
- Avoid *is when* and *is where* definitions.
- Use terms that may be familiar your reader.

Example

Most of the reading and writing required for successful life and work is transactive. Transactive writing is produced "to get something done" in the world (e.g., to provide ideas and information for a variety of purposes, to persuade readers to support a point of view). Well-educated individuals are effective readers of transactive writing and communicate information in this manner.

References

Definition

A reference identifies the sources of facts or ideas and directs readers to further information on the topic.

Tips for Creating and Using References

Writers are obligated to provide documentation for the sources of information they use. This credit for the work of others should be included in both a bibliographic list of sources and textual references to the list. An overview of a few documentation possibilities is listed below.

- Refer in a sentence to the source of the information: "According to . . . "
- Place a reference number in parentheses after the work cited: (1), (2), . . .
- Place the word reference or the abbreviation Ref. in parentheses with a number: (Reference 1).
- Write the reference number as a superscript: . . . [1]
- Identify a source for further information: (See also . . .).
- Include the author's name, full title, and publication information, if available.

Reference systems vary so widely from one field of study to another that it is impossible to provide comprehensive guidelines for all possible alternatives.

Example

As we grow older, our need for being the center of attention lessens. We no longer volunteer at family gatherings to perform our dance recital routine, nor do we replay over and over catching the fly ball in the Little League Championship game. Chemical changes in our brains, which are part of the aging process, are responsible for our feeling more embarrassed in social settings. The Better Homes and Gardens *writer Mary Conroy reported that it is much easier to stand in front of groups when you're 5 than when you're 25.*

Quotations

Definition

A quotation is the exact words of another with an acknowledgment of the source.

Tips for Creating and Using Quotations

- Cite brief, relevant passages to support key ideas.
- Avoid using quotes longer than one paragraph.
- Include only quotations that add meaning or provide necessary information.
- Provide some context for quoted material.
- Document any summary, paraphrase, or quotation that is not common knowledge, found in many sources, or your own conclusions.
- Represent the original material accurately and honestly.
- Follow rules for correct inclusion: Enclose four lines or fewer in quotation marks and separate them from the rest of the sentence with correct punctuation; separate material longer than five lines from the body of the text by indenting and single spacing, omitting quotation marks; if the quotation begins in midsentence, do not capitalize the first word.

Example

Achieving success is dependent as much on attitude as on skill. We see the truth of this phenomenon daily in those around us. Many who are skillful and knowledgeable about their craft fail to attain the pinnacles of others who have more faith in their own abilities. Henry Ford's motto should serve as a reminder to us all: *"Whether you think you can or whether you think you can't, you're right."*

ASSESSING THE EFFECTIVE USE OF PURPOSEFUL DETAILS

To assess the appropriate use of purposeful details, provide adequate time for students to return to their working folders to reexamine any previously drafted pieces in which purposeful details support would enhance the depth of idea development and audience awareness. When students complete revision for purposeful details, review their revisions to provide appropriate feedback.

If students have not yet written pieces requiring specific purposeful details support, these would be effective writing-to-learn activities for the students to place in a learning log, writer's notebook, or working folder.

CHAPTER SUMMARY

Purposeful details should be addressed as a part of the informative or technical reading-writing component of a standards-based curriculum. In most classrooms, the teaching opportunity for these support strategies exists in conjunction with research and inquiry projects of many types. As students reference a variety of sources to gain information, they should be encouraged to use these sources as models for their own writing.

This chapter provides teachers with specific examples of purposeful details used as support. This type of support, perhaps more than any other, produces a concrete connection for the reader. An effective writer considers what types of purposeful details most effectively develop ideas. When the writer carefully considers the placement and use of details such as these during prewriting and drafting, the amount of time spent on revision can be reduced. Writing given this forethought will be more successful in communicating the purpose concisely, clearly, and completely to readers.

Description

4

Description does for writing what a strand of pearls does for a simple black dress. It takes something dull and lifeless and gives it panache. In all forms of writing, descriptive passages are used to develop ideas. Though the purpose, audience, and form all dictate to some degree the type of description a writer uses, the function of this strategy does not change. It is to clarify and convey information accurately.

A writer uses rich, pertinent description—literary or technical—to fully engage the senses of intended readers. After careful analysis of both purpose and audience, a writer determines which type of descriptive development will best meet the readers' needs. In expressive and literary and some transactive writing, writers develop ideas by recreating impressions through rich, illustrative language. Ideas that are more technical and practical are developed descriptively with specific, pertinent vocabulary.

Description used for the sake of elaboration alone is a waste of a reader's time. When using description to develop ideas, writers should answer the following questions: Is the description necessary to the purpose? Does the idea warrant description? Is description the most effective way to develop the idea?

If writers choose to develop ideas descriptively, they understand that although language is key to description, economy of language is what makes it successful. Generalities and other empty verbiage convolute meaning and impede the reader's understanding. Well-chosen nouns and verbs with strong sensory connotations can reduce the need for adjectives and adverbs.

Description seldom occurs in isolated passages, except in long works. Instead, we find it interwoven in other types of support. Dialogue passages, cause-and-effect relationships, and comparison-and-contrast sequences are often laced with description. Vignette and anecdote development relies heavily on it as well. Regardless of the type of writing in which we find it, effective description enriches the message communicated.

As students learn to use description in their writing, they should adhere to the basic tenet, "Less is more." Description should not overpower writing or assault the senses, but rather, should be as subtle as that strand of pearls on the simple black dress.

TEACHING STUDENTS TO USE DESCRIPTION

Description is a clear word picture creating a sharply etched image, which provides the characteristics or qualities of an object, person, scene, event, or situation. Two types of description, referred to in most texts, are *practical* or *technical* and *subjective.* Rarely is description found in pure form; instead, it enriches all genres.

Characteristics of Description

- Supports the writer's purpose
- Meets specific needs by adding necessary information for reader
- Clarifies the ideas being developed
- Emphasizes either directly or indirectly the five senses
- Answers questions such as, "What does it look like?" or "What does it feel like?"

Supporting and Expanding Idea Development

Description supports main ideas and expands thinking by

- Building toward one dominant impression (purpose)
- Developing those specifics that support the purpose
- Establishing and maintaining a single, consistent tone and mood
- Including details that communicate the established tone and mood
- Transferring a mental image from the writer's mind to the reader's
- Articulating specifics concisely and clearly

UNDERSTANDING THE USE OF DESCRIPTION

The purpose of the learning activities in this chapter is to teach an idea development strategy for students to apply independently. When students have a clear understanding of the uses of description as support for idea development, the teacher, during written or face-to-face conferencing, may suggest this device to add depth. Students should record writing-to-learn activities from the following mini-lessons in a learning log or writer's notebook for later reference.

Mini-Lesson—Nouns and Descriptors

1. Discuss the five senses with students and ask them to provide examples using each. Have available items such as the following to allow students to experience particular senses: sandpaper, cotton balls, a whistle to blow, an onion, an orange, a flashlight, sweet-sour candy, and so on. Give students opportunities to respond and react to these sensory stimuli. You may choose to use other sensory activities that work well for students. The important thing is that students understand the different ways they respond to a variety of stimuli.

2. List on the board adjectives or adverbs that could be used to describe the various items and responses used in Activity 1. As a group, select the best one or two words or phrases to describe each. Instruct students to select the clearest, most concise words or phrases to describe the objects and sounds. Reference a grammar text for further explanation of selecting appropriate adjectives or adverbs.

3. Define for students imprecise (general) and precise (specific) nouns and pronouns. Provide examples and ask students to do the same, for example, paper—stationery, newspaper; car—convertible, Ford Taurus; she—mother, 4th-grader, my friend Sally. Call to students' attention that the use of a precise noun will often eliminate the need for an adjective. Point out that adjectives can be used to describe abstract as well as concrete nouns; however, they should be used sparingly. You may wish to reference your grammar text for further explanation of abstract and concrete nouns.

4. Refer to the lists of adjectives and adverbs generated in Activity 2 and determine specific nouns that could be described by those words. The following is an example of a student-generated response: The sandpaper might feel *rough* to the touch. Other nouns that could be described as rough might include a man's beard, a dog's tongue, ocean waves breaking on the beach, or a day at school when things did not go too well. The beam from a flashlight might be described as *bright*. This

adjective might also describe a student who does well in school, the daylight after exiting a dark cave, the North Star in the night sky, or someone's future. The sound of the whistle as it is blown could be described as *shrill, piercing,* or *loud.*

5. Ask students to look in their working folders at previously generated pieces of work to generate lists of imprecise nouns or pronouns they have used in their own writing and brainstorm possibilities for precise substitutes. Selected imprecise nouns or pronouns should be replaced by best-choice substitutions. You may also wish to encourage the careful use of meaning-making adjectives.

Mini-Lesson—Precise and Imprecise Verbs

1. Define for students imprecise (general) and precise (specific) verbs. Provide a few examples and ask students to do the same, for example, go—fly, drive, ride; run—charge, dash; walk—sneak, tiptoe; said—screamed, shouted, whispered. Call to students' attention that the use of a precise verb will often eliminate the need for an adverb. Refer to the items discussed in Mini-Lesson—Nouns and Descriptors Activity 2. Have students generate a list of precise verbs that would best describe the action of these items. The following are examples of student-generated responses: The sandpaper might be used to rub, sand, smooth, or scratch an object. The flashlight might shine or illuminate. The whistle might tweet, blast, or blare.

2. After discussing the use of precise verbs, instruct students to return to their working folders of previously drafted pieces of writing to generate lists of imprecise verbs they have used in their own writing. Once these verbs have been identified, students should brainstorm possibilities for precise substitutes and replace their imprecise verbs with best-choice substitutions. You may also wish to encourage the careful use of meaning-making adverbs. These lists of imprecise nouns and verbs and their more precise counterparts may then be posted on the wall or added to student working folders for later reference.

Mini-Lesson—"Show Me" Rather Than "Tell Me"

1. Introduce the concept of "show me" versus "tell me" sentences by reading passages that communicate images or responses through the effective use of language rather than through simple statements of fact.

Example

I began my sophomore year at a statuesque height of 5'4" and a svelte 116 pounds, but more important, the status of "new girl" catapulted me into the world of popularity. Suddenly I was the girl every boy wanted to date. Girls who were my friends were "in." I rode the coattails of this newfound popularity like a beauty queen waving from the back of a cherry-apple-red Sting Ray convertible.

2. To assist students as they identify and analyze show-me sentences, ask them to respond to questions such as the following, which reflect suggested responses to the above example.

- What important information have you gained about the character's feelings? (She was glad she looked better and was popular.)
- How do you know? (She talked about popularity and having dates and friends and compared herself to a beauty queen.)
- What language did the writer use to help you "see" or understand this? *(Statuesque, svelte, world of popularity, "in," a cherry-apple-red Sting Ray convertible.)*

3. On the board or an overhead transparency, write a tell-me sentence such as "It was cold." Ask students to generate a list of images of which they are reminded. Select one of the images generated by the students and ask questions regarding who, what, when, where, why, and how. From the responses to these questions, draft a sentence that is more of a show-me sentence than the original. Eliminating *it* or *I* will often be useful. As students revise the drafted sentence, encourage the use of precise nouns and verbs. Continue with revision until students are satisfied that the final product is a definite show-me sentence.

4. Ask students to look in their working folders at previously drafted pieces of writing and with a partner to identify "telling" sentences. Share some of these sentences with the whole class. Students will then revise their own identified sentences to create more effective "showing" sentences. You may also want students to write some of their better "showing" sentences on sentence strips to display in the classroom or to identify passages in their readings.

SUBJECTIVE AND PRACTICAL OR TECHNICAL DESCRIPTION

To this point in the lessons about description, students have learned to think generally about this idea development strategy. The terms *subjective* and *practical* or *technical* define its more specific and complex aspects. To communicate their ideas successfully, sophisticated writers will want to understand the differences between these terms and how they relate to purpose and audience. When writers create descriptions of people, places, or things, they should determine if the purpose and audience require practical/technical or subjective details or a combination of both. Practical or technical description emphasizes clear, factual information and its elaboration or interpretation for the reader. In some cases, it may include literary devices. Subjective description conveys the feelings and impressions of the writer for the reader's response and interpretation. Subjective description may also be developed by a writer's use of certain figurative language devices.

Examples

Practical or technical—*With two seconds left, the forward received a pass from the point guard. She turned and successfully attempted a 12-foot jump shot. As the buzzer sounded, the scoreboard recorded our loss 88-89.*

Subjective—*During the last seconds of the ball game, I felt as though time stood still as I watched the ball sail through the air. When it ripped the net, all hopes of victory vanished with the sound of the game-ending buzzer. My feelings mirrored those of the team as they filed silently out of the gym.*

When writing scientifically or historically, writers are expected to provide their readers with descriptions that best conform to the context. Precise and effective language are essential in meeting expectations. The following example has been analyzed and annotated to explain the interdependency of facts and description in practical or informative writing.

The tree's worst enemy is fire (fact), *and even a small fire will damage its root system, which lies close to the soil surface* (practical/technical). *Although few insects bother the red cedar* (fact), *it is the bridging host for apple rust* (practical/technical). *As a result, orchard growers make up the minority that strive to rid the area* (fact) *of these tough, stalwart, and often picturesque trees* (subjective).

Ineffective writers often supply readers with the facts only. They often fail to provide the practical or technical or subjective description required to establish connections for the reader. The preceding example, without appropriate description, might appear as follows. Notice the difference in the depth of thinking (idea development) communicated.

The tree's worst enemy is fire. Few insects bother the red cedar. Orchard growers make up the minority, striving to rid the area of these trees.

Mini-Lesson—Subjective and Practical or Technical Description

1. Provide a photograph depicting a scene that students may describe both practically or technically and subjectively. Ask them to make two separate lists of details. For the first, they will note only exactly what they see in the photo; for the second, they will list the feelings they experience when looking at the photo. News magazines are good sources for photos of, for example, the aftermath of a natural disaster, an accident scene, or a nature scene.

2. After examining the information derived from the pictures and looking at the samples above, students will write an account of the following depicted event from two perspectives and for different audiences.

Examples

(a) Your home has been burglarized and vandalized. Write a description of what has taken place for the police and another for a friend.

(b) At school you have witnessed a fight. Write a description of the fight for the principal to include in the files and another for the parents of the students involved.

(c) Write a description of your school for a Chamber of Commerce informational brochure and another for a friend who might be attending your school next year.

3. Students will analyze each example and determine which of their two descriptions is practical or technical and which is subjective description. This is a good place to reinforce the importance of audience with regard to any writing. Discuss with the class how writing for a different audience with different needs affects the way a writer approaches a purpose. Record the differences and similarities noted for future reference.

4. Students will return to their working folders and with a partner look for previously generated pieces where their writing would be enhanced by the addition of either practical/technical or subjective description. Share some of these in small groups before students revise their own work to provide more thinking or depth for the audience.

Subjective description is found most often in expressive and literary writing. Writers sometimes employ figurative language devices to evoke certain responses from their readers. Examined below are some of these devices, which may be useful to students in their development as proficient writers.

Mini-Lesson—Figurative Language

Define *figurative language* for students and discuss its use in description. You may wish to reference grammar or literature texts for a more extensive discussion and application of the following figurative language devices. Ask students to think of other examples for each of the types of figurative language which follow for verbal sharing and to locate examples from their reading to share with the class. For a contrasting view, ask students to locate samples in their science, social studies, or other texts to share. Discuss the reasons for the absence or limited use of these literary devices in these texts. In their writer's notebooks, students write examples of each of these specific figurative language examples for later reference.

1. An *analogy* develops an idea by comparing something difficult to understand with something easy to understand. To develop the analogy, a writer may create an extended metaphor. The comparison is woven throughout an entire passage, rather than included as one statement of comparison. In the extended metaphor below, growing up is compared with riding a roller-coaster:

Growing up is like riding a roller coaster. Starting out slowly, you wait and wait for something of significance to happen. Slowly, your life evolves as you climb toward monumental events or milestones. Up the hill you climb, filled with anticipation and dread. Just when you are satisfied with achieving a goal, you are plunged into a new world. At times, you feel the bottom has dropped out. Once again you climb toward a milestone, only to be met with twists and turns that alter your preconceived plan and hide what lies ahead. White-knuckled, you attempt to hold on while you are carried forward, shouting alternately with delight and fear.

2. A *metaphor* is a comparison of two unlike things in which no comparison words (*like* or *as*) are used. *My little brother is a monster.* Obviously, no little brother is a monster; but many little brothers behave like monsters, thus laying the basis for the comparison that creates a frame of reference for a reader.

3. A *simile* is a comparison of two unlike things using words of comparison (*like* or *as*). *My mother is as angry as a charging bull.* Although most readers have never witnessed a charging bull, they can make a visual reference based on prior knowledge, thus understanding the implication being made about the mother.

4. *Personification* is a literary device in which an animal, object, or idea is given the characteristics of a human personality. *That stubborn zipper refused to budge.* There is no way that of its own accord a zipper could budge, but readers understand the connotation of the verb *budge* and can make the connection to a zipper that is stuck and will not move.

5. *Onomatopoeia* is the use of a word the sound of which suggests its meaning. *The ball swooshed through the net.* A reader makes the connection between the word *swoosh* and the swoosh sound the basketball makes as it passes through the net. Onomatopoeia can also be a poetic device.

6. Three literary devices involve the repetition of letter sounds. *Alliteration,* also a poetic device, is the repetition of initial consonant sounds in closely clustered words. *The babbling brook broke through the bowed branches. Assonance* is the repetition of vowel sounds without the repetition of consonants. *I seldom find time to be silent. Consonance* is repetition of consonant sounds not limited to the first letter of each word. *The checkered tablecloth was rounded at the corners.*

7. A *hyperbole* is an exaggeration or overstatement. *My dad had a cow when he saw my grades.* Of course, there is no way that anyone's father actually gave birth to a cow, but the familiarity of hyperboles aids a reader in understanding their mean-

ings. Many hyperboles have become so familiar as English vernacular that they are classified as clichés. Although clichés may reinforce ideas, they are often ineffective for development of ideas.

8. Ask students to look in their working folders with a partner to identify places where their writing would be enhanced by the addition of any of the preceding figurative language devices. Share some of these in small groups before students make revisions to their work to provide more thinking and depth for an audience.

UNDERSTANDING APPLICATIONS IN WRITING

1. Have students analyze the description models found at the end of this chapter to identify characteristics of description (see the "Characteristics of Description" list above). Discuss how this support enhances the ideas being developed and helps communicate the purpose to a reader. Once students are able to analyze the models, provide readings from a variety of sources to identify passages where writers have used description to develop ideas. Examples are readily accessible in such publications as newspapers, magazines, and journals.

2. Copy passages containing description that were located by students and ask them to highlight the specific descriptive segments. To check for understanding, examine these in groups or post selections in the room. Read and examine the student-selected descriptive segments. Discuss how they enhance the writer's purpose (see "Supporting and Expanding Idea Development" at the beginning of this chapter). After highlighting descriptive segments, some students may identify the segments as practical/technical or as subjective description. Students will then determine how the different kinds of description are successful in communicating the purpose to the reader.

3. The following questions may be used to assist students in analyzing the use of description:

♦ What necessary information does this description provide?
♦ What image is conveyed through the description; how does it *show* rather than *tell?*
♦ What language (precise nouns or verbs, figurative language, etc.) creates the image?
♦ Which senses are emphasized?
♦ How does this description support the writer's purpose?

4. Ask students to select one piece of literary or expressive writing from their working folders. Using the skills acquired during these lessons, students will revise the piece to add depth to the idea development for the reader. After revising

the literary or expressive piece of writing, have students return it to their working folder and select one piece of writing that is more content specific and make similar revisions to it.

ASSESSING THE EFFECTIVE USE OF DESCRIPTION

As teachers or peers assess the application of description in student writing, the following criteria should be addressed. General descriptions:

- ❑ Support the focused purpose of the writing and the main idea of the paragraph by building toward one dominant impression
- ❑ Establish and communicate a consistent tone and mood
- ❑ Transfer a mental image from the writer's mind to the reader's
- ❑ Allow the reader to experience the scene through meaning-making language such as "showing" sentences and language; precise nouns, verbs, adjectives, and adverbs; sensory details or figurative language

Subjective descriptions:

- ❑ Convey the feelings and impressions of the writer
- ❑ Allow for elaboration and interpretation by the reader

Practical descriptions:

- ❑ Emphasize clear, factual information
- ❑ Provide elaboration or interpretation for the reader
- ❑ (May) include literary devices

EXAMPLES OF DESCRIPTION TO BE USED AS CLASSROOM MODELS

Students will benefit from recognizing and examining description as it appears in different forms of writing. The following examples are included to provide additional classroom models. To ensure that students have internalized the concept and will make successful application in their own writing, they must be afforded many opportunities to locate and consider the effectiveness of different types of description used for support. This need not be an added burden for the teacher, but rather should be an integral part of reading instruction that encourages students to think critically about their reading as well as their writing. Description support is denoted by italics.

Examples of precise language (nouns, verbs, etc.) are found throughout the following subjectively described setting:

> As in stories, my childhood was the days when *the stillness of night could be felt creeping toward me* (metaphor) *like the midnight fog* (simile) while I lay in *the dew-carpeted* (metaphor) *grass.* It *was the nights the crickets chirped to me and sang their sweet melodies* (metaphor and personification) as the air was chilled just enough so that my breath was frosted as it floated upward. The *burning afternoons under a shade of a friendly tree* (personification) and a wade in the *cool creek* (alliteration) were *those days of my youth, all from a storybook* (metaphor).
>
> (12th-Grade Student)

> To some people in the world, French is a language only spoken by *high-class men in suits or by pompous waiters* (subjective description). In others' opinions, *French is a language spoken only by the French themselves and cannot be used outside of France* (subjective description). Though these assumptions are widespread and common, they are simply not true. Despite all of the current disbeliefs and misrepresentations of the French language, *this centuries-old art of communication* (practical or technical description) *is one of the most active languages in the world today* (subjective description). Contradictory to present suppositions, *French is a global language* (practical or technical), *plays a crucial role in the business world, and is an opportunity not to pass up when registering for high school courses* (subjective description).
>
> (12th-Grade Student)

> *The Die Block Assembly consists of two machined block sections, eight Code Punch Pins, and a Feed Punch Pin. The larger section, called the Die Block, is fashioned of a hard, non-corrosive beryllium-copper alloy.* (In this example, figurative language devices are absent; most content-specific writing employs practical or technical description.)
>
> (Shelton, 1994, p. 139)

The following examples contain no annotations and may be used for student analysis:

> *His entrance is with a limp, caused by the angry bruises on his shin and knee—the gift of a cow that did not want to be in the chute. Smashed nails and split fingertips are doctored daily and then, of necessity, mistreated again. The physical pain and the weariness seem to be a normal part of the responsibilities of daily life.*
>
> (7th-Grade Student)

In 1980, half our rainforests were destroyed and now less than five percent are left for us to utilize. *A very interesting fact is that in about the time it takes you to tie your shoelaces (one-minute), sixty acres of rainforest are destroyed!* Sixty acres equals about twenty football fields. *This gives me chills just thinking about everything that we are losing: the world's medicine cabinet and unthinkable amounts of animals and plants.*

(4th-Grade Student)

Black light has been used to create dramatic effects for many years. *Dancers in the 1930s performed in theaters in New York City wearing white gloves that appeared to move by themselves in midair. The rest of the dancers' costumes were invisible on a darkened stage.*

(12th-Grade Student)

CHAPTER SUMMARY

Description is one of the most misused idea development strategies in student writing. Lack of understanding with regard to the effective use of description often leads inexperienced writers to overuse adjectives and adverbs to describe weak nouns and verbs. Teaching description strategies in the manner suggested in this chapter will assist student writers as they make decisions about their writing. Since purposeful communication with an audience is the guiding element in standards-based writing instruction, teachers must encourage students to think critically about description in order to communicate ideas effectively.

Comparison and Contrast

5

Comparisons allow the reader to make connections between similarities; contrasts prepare the reader to understand differences. Unlike some other idea development strategies, which can stand alone, a comparison or a contrast relationship requires much more complex development.

A writer often draws on more simplistic strategies (e.g., facts, practical or subjective description, analogy, similes, etc.) to successfully set up comparison or contrast relationships. Ideas developed through such relationships provide readers with contexts for understanding information. The paragraph below develops the idea that Mark McGwire now holds the unblemished single season home run record. Facts are used to establish comparisons and contrasts between Roger Maris's and McGwire's records.

> On Wednesday, September 8, 1998, at 8:18 p.m. Eastern Standard Time, St. Louis Cardinals' first baseman Mark McGwire hit his 62nd home run, breaking the 37-year-old record held by Roger Maris of the New York Yankees. Maris was the first to break the 60-run record previously held by baseball legend Babe Ruth. Though Maris was credited with the new record, his feat was shadowed because it was accomplished in 162 games to Ruth's 154. McGwire's record will not have to carry such a disclaimer. He surpassed the mark in his 145th game, played at Busch Stadium where, ironically, Roger Maris played his final professional baseball game as a St. Louis Cardinal.

Thoughtful writers carefully analyze the intended audience before developing an idea through comparisons or contrasts. If the purpose of using this type of development is to present new information, the writer will connect the new information to the reader's prior knowledge. If readers have no context to which the new information can be compared or contrasted, they cannot make the connection.

57

For example, if writers wish to explain the concept of democracy to local elementary school children, they would not choose to compare or contrast our current form of government with that of Iraq. A more appropriate choice might be comparing and contrasting decisions made by parents without children's input to those where children are included in the decision-making process. Although young children have very little knowledge of foreign governments, they do understand family synergy.

As writers become more sophisticated, they seek methods that subtly communicate their thinking. Whether the writing is technical or expressive, ideas developed through comparison and contrast provide readers with essential thinking connections.

TEACHING STUDENTS TO USE COMPARISON AND CONTRAST

Comparing or contrasting two or more things, people, processes, events, or concepts is accomplished by noting points of both similarity and difference between them. Comparisons generally place the greater emphasis on similarities, whereas contrasts particularly stress differences. Comparison and contrast is a basic method of looking at things closely.

Example

From the start, Ashlea's and Alison's personalities differed in many respects. Ashlea was adventurous and determined; Alison's nature was more easygoing and content. Both of them, however, have become confident, successful adults.

Characteristics of Comparison and/or Contrast

- Supports the writer's purpose
- Provides a frame of reference for the reader
- Helps the reader choose between alternatives
- Acquaints readers with the difficult or unfamiliar by relating it to something simpler or more familiar

---

Supporting and Expanding Idea Development

Comparing and/or contrasting support main ideas and expand thinking by:

- Selecting comparisons and contrasts appropriate for the readership
- Emphasizing the point of the writing
- Comparing and contrasting comparable things
- Establishing a basis for the comparison or contrast
- Presenting many possibilities and interpretations for the reader
- Pointing out specific parallels or differences between things compared
- Providing enough elaboration of pertinent comparisons and contrasts

UNDERSTANDING THE CONCEPT OF COMPARISON AND CONTRAST

The purpose of the learning activities in this chapter is to teach an idea development strategy for students to apply independently. When students have a clear understanding of the uses of comparison and contrast as support for idea development, the teacher, during written or face-to-face conferencing, may suggest this strategy to add depth. Students should record writing-to-learn activities from the following mini-lessons in a learning log or writer's notebook for later reference.

1. Show students objects or people with similarities, for example, coins, textbooks, maps, computers, physical education equipment, students, and any others you may wish to include. Have students identify the similarities and differences in common items and then examine similarities and differences in items of their choosing.

2. Using one classroom example, instruct the class to examine items by creating expanded lists of similarities or differences. Push the thinking of students for greater fluency and diversity.

Example

Compare a Canadian $20 coin and the Susan B. Anthony $1 coin.

Similarities	*Differences*
Image of a woman	Different women
Monetary value	Different values
Round shape	Different sizes
Different image on back and front	One gold, one silver

3. Use the questions below to expand the thinking about the similarities and differences generated. Consider the different purposeful details writers employ to communicate ideas to the reader (e.g., lists, descriptions, definitions, narrations, and illustrations).

◆ What other information is needed to fully understand this similarity or difference? (Queen Elizabeth II is on the Canadian $20 coin; Susan B. Anthony is on the $1. Both were significant figures in their countries' histories, though for different reasons. Queen Elizabeth II is living; Susan B. Anthony is not.)

◆ What details would someone benefit from knowing about this similarity or difference? (The $20 Canadian coin is not valid currency in the United States. Queen Elizabeth II is a current reigning monarch in Great Britain; Susan B. Anthony was a leader in the woman's suffrage movement in the United States.)

◆ Why is this information needed to understand the similarity or difference? (Based on weight, the actual value of the Canadian coin may exceed $20 in the United States. Ironically, though Queen Elizabeth II is the most recognized public figure in Great Britain today and is on this coin, she has no political or governmental powers. Although Susan B. Anthony does not have the name recognition of Queen Elizabeth II, her efforts to win the right for women to vote impact our lives each day.)

Notice that these responses allow students to examine the similarities and differences they have generated at a deeper thinking level. After this analysis, students may more easily determine those similarities or differences that are most significant in establishing depth and complexity of ideas for an audience. Merely listing superficial similarities or differences, such as size and shape, would add little, if any, importance to the development of ideas.

4. Ask students to return to the lists of similarities and differences generated earlier. Expand their thinking about similarities and differences by recording responses to questions similar to those suggested above. Using the subject matter in their other courses or significant activities or events in their own lives as a basis, students will develop lists of possible purposes for writing comparisons and contrasts, listing points necessary to include and purposeful details (e.g. description, illustrations, narration) to develop the points.

UNDERSTANDING APPLICATIONS IN WRITING

1. Have students analyze the models of comparison-and-contrast support located at the end of this chapter. Discuss how this support enhances the ideas being developed and helps to communicate the purpose to the reader. Once students understand the analysis process, have them locate and analyze examples

from contemporary writing or classroom readings to identify comparison or contrast support. Provide enough examples and discussion to allow students to recognize this relationship.

To check for understanding, ask students to bring in written examples that feature comparison or contrast support and identify the purpose of each comparison or contrast.

2. Students may use the following questions to assist them as they analyze the comparison or contrast relationship in the written samples.

♦ What are the similarities or differences noted?
♦ What purposeful details (e.g., narration, description, or definition) does the writer use to elaborate the pertinent comparisons or contrasts to help the reader understand?
♦ What possibilities and interpretations does the comparison or contrast present?
♦ How does the comparison or contrast support emphasize the writer's point?
♦ How does this comparison or contrast add to the reader's understanding of the idea being developed and the focused purpose of the piece?
♦ What transitional devices indicate the comparison or contrast relationship? Students should apply their general knowledge of transitions to this type of idea development. Certain transitions, such as *however, in contrast to, compared to, on the other hand, in addition to,* are most often used to move the reader through the thinking in this type of idea development.

3. Select one of the following purposes to be developed by comparison or contrast support (or use one of your own) to share on the board or an overhead transparency. *A person's work habits directly influence his or her success. Organisms have basic needs and survive in environments where their needs are met. Human and physical characteristics give a place meaning and change over time. The interpretation of an historical event may change as new information is uncovered.* Ask students to use the questions below to analyze their chosen purpose.

♦ What similarities and differences could support the purpose?
♦ What other information is needed to fully understand the similarities or differences?
♦ What details would someone benefit from knowing about similarities or differences?
♦ Why would this information be important to understanding the significance of the similarities or differences selected?

4. Check to be certain that all students have moved to understanding and application of comparison or contrast support used to develop ideas that communicate a purpose. This step moves students beyond examining concrete ideas, as in the coins example, to more abstract concepts.

APPLICATIONS TO WRITING

1. As a whole group, generate a list of possible writing topics applicable to the content being taught or refer to previously prepared lists in learning logs or writer's notebooks. After selecting a topic, each student will determine a focused purpose to address and decide on an audience appropriate for the topic. Once the purpose has been determined, students will examine ideas that support the purpose.

2. Students will select one idea to develop using comparison or contrast support. If students have difficulty developing this idea through comparison or contrast support, ask them to select another that is more appropriate for this type of development.

3. Have students form small groups based on similar topics and share the developed idea for analysis by using the following questions:

- ◆ What commonalties do you see in the development of the ideas?
- ◆ Which comparisons or contrasts provide the strongest support?
- ◆ Which comparisons or contrasts (if any) do not provide enough information for the reader to understand the relationship?
- ◆ Identify transitional devices (language) in the sentences that indicate the comparison or contrast relationship.

Students should apply their general knowledge of transitions to this type of idea development. Certain transitions, such as *however, in contrast to, compared to,* or *on the other hand,* are most often used to move the reader through the thinking in this type of development. Students will require teacher feedback regarding the effectiveness of their idea development and its analysis. Provide adequate time for students to return to their working folders to reexamine previously drafted pieces, looking for places where comparison or contrast support would add depth or audience awareness.

ASSESSING THE EFFECTIVE USE OF COMPARISON AND CONTRAST

As teachers or peers assess the application of comparison and contrast in student writing, the following criteria should be addressed. Comparisons and contrasts must:

- ❏ Support the focused purpose of the writing and the main idea of the paragraph
- ❏ Provide a frame of reference for the reader
- ❏ Help the reader choose between alternatives
- ❏ Acquaint the reader with the difficult or unfamiliar by relating it to the simple or familiar
- ❏ Be appropriate for the readership

❑ Compare and contrast comparable things
❑ Present various possibilities and interpretations for the reader
❑ Point out specific parallels or differences
❑ Provide elaboration

EXAMPLES OF COMPARISON AND CONTRAST TO BE USED AS CLASSROOM MODELS

Students will benefit from recognizing and examining passages that contain comparison-and-contrast support as they appear in different forms of writing. The following examples are included to provide additional classroom models. To ensure that students have internalized the concepts and will successfully apply them in their own writing, they must be afforded many opportunities to locate and consider the effectiveness of comparisons and contrasts used for support. This need not be an added burden for the teacher, but rather should be an integral part of reading instruction that encourages students to think critically about their reading as well as their writing. Passages including comparison and contrast support are denoted by italics.

> *The dolphin is often confused, even by scientists and fishermen, with its look-alike, the porpoise.* But a close look shows important differences. *The dolphin's teeth are cone-like and pointed, rather than spade-shaped like the porpoise's. A dolphin's dorsal fin is curved toward the tail, while most porpoises have triangular fins. And the dolphin has a much larger brain than its porpoise relative.* That is where the intelligence that so interests its other relative, humankind, is stored. (Contrast)
>
> (*Scope English,* 1987, p. 122)

> You could walk just about anywhere you wanted on Mars, because the entire surface is land; there are no lakes, rivers, or oceans. All the water is underground or frozen at the north and south poles. *There's as much land on Mars as there is on Earth, even though Mars is only half as big as Earth and weighs only a tenth as much. Because of its weaker gravity, Mars is not as dense as Earth; it's puffed up.* (Comparison and contrast)
>
> (Darrach & Petranek, 1995, pp. 116-117)

> An old woman with white, curly hair is passing out presents. She is wearing a beautiful, purple pleated dress. *In size she compares to Aunt Anne, thin and straight.* Her face is attractive and understanding. Her eyes are gray and sunken in; they twinkle like jewels. (Comparison)
>
> (4th-Grade Student)

In a couple of hours my brother and I started off to the sledding hill. *This wasn't like walking through any old snow.* This was twenty heavy inches of ice and snow. (Contrast)

(4th-Grade Student)

The kind of fat we eat also effects *[sic]* our cholesterol levels. Diets high in saturated fat can raise cholesterol levels. Saturated fats are usually solid at room temperature. *When saturated fats such as bacon or steak grease are left on the kitchen counter for a while, they will turn white and hard. This is how you can visually tell it is a saturated fat. If vegetable oil, like corn or sunflower oil, is left out at room temperature it stays liquid.* Vegetable oil is the best kind of oil to use in cooking. (Contrast)

(7th-Grade Student)

My mother had warned me about Arrow. She and Elsie had been inseparable companions since birth. Somewhere along the line, though, *Elsie had grown up a little faster than Arrow. Although they both lived on the ranch, Elsie also had a house in the city where she could commute to the business of civilization. Since Arrow's parents were struggling potters, she was confined to the ranch. For several years Arrow had been helping with the kiln and clay while Elsie was busy developing and growing. Arrow was responsible but not experienced.* (Comparison and contrast)

(12th-Grade Student)

Through the entire creation of this masterpiece, da Vinci was much like today's youth, working with music and other deliberate noise in the background. He even had the television of the times, a reader of great poetry chatting away. Perhaps these amenities were meant to soothe the experience for la Gioconda, perhaps he sought inspiration from the music and words, . . . we'll never know, will we? (Comparison)

(12th-Grade Student)

CHAPTER SUMMARY

Comparison-and-contrast thinking does not exist in isolation, but as a part of a larger piece of work. In a similar manner, seldom will a reader encounter a paragraph developed solely through the use of comparisons or contrasts. Instead, effective comparison-and-contrast thinking should establish a context for the reader to more clearly understand a writer's overall purpose or a paragraph's main idea.

Activities in this chapter will assist students in thinking through and developing comparison-and-contrast support beyond a superficial reference. To develop a comparison or contrast relationship effectively, a writer must successfully employ other idea development strategies such as facts or practical or subjective description.

Through focused attention during instruction, students learn to critically assess writing situations where comparison-and-contrast support will enhance their finished product. To achieve expected local, state, and national standards, such specificity of instructional practice is essential.

6 ◆ Cause and Effect

Writing develops as one thought leads to another and then another—the natural way a writer moves a reader through a piece of writing. This cause-and-effect reasoning is woven through all kinds of writing and is often the basis for other types of support. In student writing, at all developmental levels, we see attempts at cause-and-effect reasoning to support purposes. Many of these attempts are unsuccessful, however, because inexperienced writers often lack the necessary analysis and reasoning skills.

As experienced writers develop ideas to support their purposes, they seldom give conscious attention to how they go about it. Inexperienced writers, however, need to make conscious decisions about their writing. Student writing improves when students learn to apply cause-and-effect reasoning as a means of idea development.

Cause-and-effect reasoning is an analysis process during which a situation may be examined from two angles. The writer's responsibility to the reader is to provide either effects for certain causes or causes for certain effects. When writers develop an idea through a cause-and-effect relationship, they enable readers to draw sound conclusions and to think logically about the idea.

Ideas are usually developed not as a single cause or effect but through a series of causes and their effects—causal chains. A causal chain occurs when the effect of a preceding cause becomes the cause for another effect. A successful causal chain includes directly connected causes and effects that correspond to each other and that continue to support the purpose. An unsuccessful causal chain overlooks a direct effect and moves to one distanced from the cause, resulting in a gap in logic.

With clear reasoning as one goal of effective writing, writers should be careful not to present something as a cause or effect for their readers when it is merely a coincidence of events. Writers should not mislead readers by presenting coincidence as primary evidence. Nor should they include causes or effects that fail to support the purpose.

Although cause and effect at first appears to be a difficult strategy to teach, actually it is a type of reasoning that is innate to all humans. From birth, we understand the powerful connection of causes and effects. When students learn the application of this thinking strategy as an idea development technique, they will produce clear, concise writing.

TEACHING STUDENTS CAUSE AND EFFECT

Definition

Cause and effect reasoning establishes a connection to explain why circumstances occurred or to examine results.

Example

> On her first trip to a large amusement park, the number of rides from which she had to choose overwhelmed Sue. As she stood in line waiting to ride the world-renowned roller-coaster, *her palms began to sweat and her mouth felt as if it were filled with hundreds of cotton balls.* So much for putting on a brave front, *she was scared and now everyone would know it.* (Effect-cause)

Characteristics of Cause and Effect

- Communicate the writer's purpose with pertinent support in the form of additional details about the cause or effect, connections between causes and effects, or elaboration about cause or effect to establish its relevance to the purpose
- Explain why or what resulted
- Establish clear, logical relationships

> **Supporting and Expanding Idea Development**
>
> Cause-and-effect explanation supports main ideas and expands thinking by:
>
> - Providing justification for actions, events, and situations
> - Avoiding fallacies in reasoning
> - Making related connections for the reader
> - Establishing the immediate or long-range consequences for actions
> - Examining various outcomes from events and situations
> - Predicting reactions to actions, events, and situations

UNDERSTANDING THE CONCEPT OF CAUSE AND EFFECT

The purpose of the learning activities in this chapter is to teach an idea development strategy for students to apply independently. When students have a clear understanding of the uses of causes and effects as support for idea development, the teacher, during written or face-to-face conferencing, may suggest using this device to add depth. Students should record writing-to-learn activities from the following mini-lessons in a learning log or writer's notebook for later reference.

1. Introduce cause and effect through some of the following activities: Light a candle, then cover it with a jar; add dishwashing liquid to water and stir it to cause bubbles; chew bubble gum and blow a bubble; slam a book to the floor or slam a door to create a loud noise; role-play a scene in which one person is angry and another reacts. Substitute or add others of your own design. In writing to demonstrate learning (of the concept), ask students to record other cause-and-effect circumstances from their own experiences. Examine their responses for understanding.

2. Students will recognize a variety of causes for the following effects: a scab on a knee, a failing grade, the revoking of privileges, opening an umbrella, closing a window, or others of your own design. In writing to demonstrate learning (of the concept), ask students to record other cause-and-effect circumstances from their own experiences. Examine their responses for understanding.

3. Students will recognize a variety of effects for the following causes: driving too fast, disobeying parents, running in the hall, going outside in the rain without a raincoat, eating ice cream too fast, or others of your own design. In writing to demonstrate learning (of the concept), ask students to record other cause circumstances from their own experiences, which may result in a variety of effects. Examine their responses for understanding.

4. Students will recognize a causal chain—one cause leading to an effect, which acts as the cause of another effect (cause [c] → effect [e] → cause [c] → effect [e]).

Example
You fall down   → you break your leg → you have a cast → you can't swim.
(cause)   (e becomes c)   (e becomes c)   (effect)

Instruct students to read first cause and last effect to identify any gaps in logic and reasoning. The following examples are for in-class practice. Discuss one for the whole class to model. Ask students to complete two more in small groups or pairs. Then ask students to complete another individually.

♦ Your alarm fails to sound   → you oversleep   → (   ) → (   )
♦ Too much rain   → flooded streams → (   ) → (   )
♦ Eating sweets   → tooth decay   → (   ) → (   )

When the causal chain no longer supports the purpose, the chain stops. In writing to demonstrate learning (of the concept), ask students to record other causal chains from their own experiences. Examine their responses for concept understanding.

UNDERSTANDING APPLICATIONS IN WRITING

In order to understand how writers develop ideas, students should examine such development within the context of whole texts. In this manner, they may more fully understand the importance of purpose and audience considerations to the writer's selections of support strategies.

Mini-Lesson—Analyzing Models

1. Have students analyze the models of cause-and-effect support located at the end of this chapter. Discuss how this support enhances the ideas being developed and helps to communicate the purpose to the reader.

2. Ask students to examine examples from some contemporary writing or classroom readings. Use the following questions to analyze the examples for application to idea development:

♦ How does (do) the effect(s) support the cause(s)?
♦ How does (do) the cause(s) support the effect(s)?

♦ How does the cause-and-effect relationship add to the reader's understanding of the idea being developed and the focused purpose of the piece?

♦ How does the cause-and-effect support provide insight for the reader to predict the actions, events, situations, or ideas that follow?

♦ What is the connection between the cause and the effect support?

♦ Do fallacies or omitted information mislead the reader or cause doubt about the purpose of the writing?

♦ What transitional devices (language) indicate the cause-and-effect relationship (e.g., *therefore, due to, can result in, because, consequently, as a result*)?

Students will highlight the transitions in samples. (Refer students to a grammar book for learning to discriminate among the transitions for different purposes. Subordinate clauses, etc. would be effective topics for mini-lessons.) Provide enough examples or discussion to allow students to recognize this relationship.

3. Ask students to bring in written examples or provide resources to locate cause-and-effect support. Students will identify and analyze the purpose of each cause and effect. Use the questions and directions in Activity 2 to analyze the examples for application to idea development.

Mini-Lesson—Revising Sentences

1. Examine the following sentence, which would be enhanced by cause-and-effect support: *The number of homeless families is increasing.*

2. Looking at the above sentence as an effect, students will generate possible causes. If students have difficulty beginning, you may wish to offer some of the following: corporate downsizing, single-parent families, lack of education, disasters. As a whole group, create sentences incorporating the generated causes with the effect.

3. Looking at the sentence in number 1 as a cause, students will generate possible effects. If students have difficulty beginning, you may wish to offer some of the following: the need for more community support facilities (homeless shelters, etc.), the increase in infant mortality, students who are underprepared for school, students who come to school hungry, and high school absentee rates. As a whole group, create sentences incorporating the generated effects with their causes.

4. In writing to demonstrate learning, ask students to create other cause-and-effect sentences from their own experiences or content from other classes. Examine the student responses for understanding of the skill. Encourage students to use responses to earlier mini-lessons in their writer's notebook.

Mini-Lesson—Creating Causal Chains

1. Examine the following sentence, which would be enhanced by cause-and-effect support: *The number of homeless families is increasing.*

2. As a whole group, students generate possible causal chains. If students have difficulty beginning, you may wish to offer some of the following: Recession → company downsizing → job lost → no rent money → homeless. Homeless → no lavatory facilities → increase in health problems → absenteeism. Job lost → no rent money → homeless → no lavatory facilities. When the causal chain no longer supports the purpose, the chain stops.

3. As a whole group, create sentences incorporating the causal chains.

4. In writing to demonstrate learning, ask students to create other causal chain sentences from their own experiences or content from other classes. Examine these for understanding of the skill. Encourage students to use responses to earlier mini-lessons in their writer's notebook.

Mini-Lesson—Analyzing Classroom Models

1. As a whole group, analyze the writing samples at the end of this chapter by identifying the following: the focused purpose for the sample; the idea that is being supported; the supporting sentences as *cause*, *effect*, or *causal chain*; transitional devices (language).

2. Discuss the success of the causes or effects as support for the idea conveyed.

Example

> One morning in 1878, a soap-factory worker returned from lunch and realized he had allowed a vat of white soap to mix too long. Too much air had been whipped into the mixture, but the worker poured it into bars and sent it out anyway.
>   Public response was immediate—everyone wanted the wonderful floating soap. When owners Harley Procter and James Gamble figured out what happened, they ordered every vat of white soap to be over-mixed. Then they came up with the perfect name: Ivory.
>   (Lassieur, 1995, p. 28)

♦ Identify the idea that is being supported. (The accidental creation of Ivory Soap)

- Identify supporting sentences as *cause, effect,* or *causal chain.*

  He had allowed a vat of white soap to mix too long. (Cause) → Too much air had been whipped into the mixture (Effect),—but the worker poured it into bars and sent it out anyway. (Cause) → Public response was immediate—everyone wanted the wonderful floating soap. (Effect) Public response was immediate—everyone wanted the wonderful floating soap. (Cause) → When owners Harley Procter and James Gamble figured out what happened, they ordered every vat of white soap to be over-mixed (Effect) (Causal chain).

- Identify transitional devices (language). *(One morning in 1878, but, immediate, when, then.* Verbs such as *realized* and *figured out* also serve a transitional function.)
- Discuss the success of causes and effects as support for the idea being conveyed. (The reader is able to follow the progression of events leading to the marketing of soap and fully understand the significance of the coincidence and its results.)

APPLICATIONS TO WRITING

The following activities are to be completed as a whole group:

1. Generate a list of possible writing topics applicable to content being taught or refer to any previously prepared lists in their learning log or writer's notebook.

2. After selecting a topic, students determine a focused purpose (Why might someone want or need to know about this topic?) and audience (Who might want or need to know?). Use an active prewriting strategy to demonstrate that one topic lends itself to many possible purposes and audiences, for example, "slice the pie" (divide the topic into many audience-purpose-form possibilities), cluster, or web for ideas and support.

3. Determine ideas that support the purpose and select one to be developed.

4. In small groups, students will compose cause-and-effect sentences to support the idea and identify each sentence as *cause, effect,* or *causal chain* form of support.

5. Groups share sentences they have composed and answer the following questions:

- What are the commonalties you see in these sentences?
- Which of the sentences provide stronger support for the idea?

♦ Which sentences (if any) do not provide enough information for the reader to follow the cause-and-effect thinking?

♦ What are the transitional devices (language) in the sentences that indicate the cause-and-effect relationship?

Students should apply their general knowledge of transitions to this particular type of idea development. Certain transitions, for example, *because of, since, so that, in order to, therefore, hence,* are most often used to move the reader through the thinking in this type of development. Students will require teacher feedback regarding the effectiveness of sentence analysis.

6. Provide adequate time for students to return to their working folders to reexamine previously drafted pieces, looking for places where cause-and-effect support would add depth or audience awareness.

7. Some students may want to develop an entire piece of writing around one of the generated ideas, whereas others may wish to use this technique for idea development in future writing. Some may choose to do nothing further with the writing generated from these activities.

ASSESSING THE EFFECTIVE USE OF CAUSE AND EFFECT

As teachers or peers assess the application of cause-and-effect support in student writing, the following criteria should be addressed. Cause and effect must:

❑ Support the purpose of the piece and main idea of the paragraph by providing additional details about the relationship, connections between causes and effects, and elaboration about the cause or effect to establish relevance
❑ Explain why or what resulted
❑ Establish clear, logical relationships
❑ Justify actions, events, or situations
❑ Avoid fallacies in reasoning
❑ Establish consequences for actions or events
❑ Make predictions concerning actions, events, situations
❑ Provide a logical outcome

EXAMPLES OF CAUSE AND EFFECT TO BE USED AS CLASSROOM MODELS

Students will benefit from recognizing and examining causes and effects as they appear in different forms of writing. The following examples are included to provide additional classroom models. To ensure that students have internalized the concept and will successfully apply it in their own writing, they must be afforded many opportunities to locate and consider the effectiveness of cause and effect used for support. This need not be an added burden for the teacher, but rather should be an integral part of reading instruction that encourages students to think critically about their reading as well as their writing. Cause-and-effect support is denoted by italics.

> From what I have read, the violin has had the same basic design for more than four hundred years. *You will see that the strings press tightly against a piece called the bridge, which transmits the vibrations of the strings to the thin belly, or soundboard.* (Cause and effect)
>
> (Lassieur, 1995, p. 28)

> One morning in 1878, a soap-factory worker returned from lunch and realized *he had allowed a vat of white soap to mix too long. Too much air had been whipped into the mixture, but the worker poured it into bars and sent it out anyway. Public response was immediate—everyone wanted the wonderful floating soap.* (Causal chain)
>
> (Lassieur, 1995, p. 28)

> To test his theory, *Pasteur decided to inject saliva from a mad animal into the brain of a dog.* He did this, *and the dog became mad. He tried the same thing with other dogs. All the dogs became mad.* At last Pasteur was satisfied that his theory had been proved. (Cause-effect, cause-effect)
>
> (Robinson & Monroe, 1970, p. 17)

> Carl Lewis should be anchoring the U.S. 4 × 100 relay on Saturday. *And if the coach of the U.S. track team doesn't want to put Lewis on that relay, he should be thanked very much for his time and told that he is no longer coaching the U.S. track team.* (Cause-effect-effect)

CHAPTER SUMMARY

The development of effective cause-and-effect relationships in writing can make the difference between a confused reader and one who is able to follow the progression of events with ease. Inexperienced writers who omit critical components of cause-and-effect relationships leave their readers with insufficient information and explanation.

In this chapter, the teacher leads student writers through a thinking and writing process designed to help eliminate cause-and-effect confusions. Although cause-and-effect reasoning is a crucial concept in all disciplines, its application in writing has not been traditionally emphasized. Therefore, although students may be cognizant of the relationship they wish to communicate, their inability to establish connections for the reader leads to the appearance of flawed thinking.

To meet local, state, and national standards, conscious critical thinking must become inherent to all instructional processes. When students learn to analyze their intentions for communicating with an audience, and when they learn effective strategies for developing ideas, sound writing will result.

Dialogue

When we speak, conversing one-to-one, we take the nuances and power of communication for granted. When we write, we must provide for the reader these same nuances and that same power through dialogue.

Dialogue captures readers, transports them into the scene in a way speechless prose cannot. It fills voids with opportunities for readers to think, interpret, or reflect. Dialogue breathes life into characters, adds the music of voices to words. Narrative writing without dialogue is the beach without a sunset or the sky without clouds.

The versatility of dialogue makes it essential for a writer's tool kit. To engage readers of both fiction and nonfiction, strong writers understand the many functions of this idea development strategy. Their scenes shout, scream, sob, pulse with life. Their characters become multidimensional, lifelike personalities to inhabit stories. Their ideas gain depth when revealed through the voices of others. The dialogue is a necessary element of their writing.

Yet conversation standing on its own contains insufficient information for a reader. Explanatory text strengthens the voices of dialogue, allowing the reader to fully perceive an experience. Dialogue is more than just words in quotation marks. For readers of fiction, a character's thoughts, movements, and motivations are often revealed through explanatory text, as are action and setting details. Nonfiction readers, too, expect explanatory text coupled with narration that further illustrates or amplifies the writer's intentions.

Experience enables writers to determine the most appropriate types of development for ideas. When a writer chooses to use dialogue, it should be purposeful: beneficial to the reader, significant to the communication, and supportive of the whole. Overuse of dialogue may produce the opposite effect. Teaching students to support and expand ideas through dialogue and accompanying text opens options to them as writers of both fiction and nonfiction.

TEACHING STUDENTS TO USE DIALOGUE

Dialogue is conversation between two or more characters. It is the basis for the existence of plays.

Example

With her hands on her hips, my mother was pacing the floor as I skulked into the kitchen. One look at her face told me all I needed to know.

She turned, her green eyes flashing with anger and hurt. "You've been with them again, haven't you?" she demanded. "How many times do I have to tell you? They don't care anything about you." Her voice rose to a shrill pitch. "They're just using you." Her pointed finger punctuated the air with every word.

Shifting my weight from foot to foot, I stammered, "But, Mom . . . " However, she allowed me no opportunity for explanation.

"How do you think I feel when you're an hour late and I can't find you anywhere?" she questioned, a pleading note in her voice.

I wrapped my arms around her frail shoulders in a hug. Then smiled, shook my head, and climbed the stairs to my room where I knew I would be for the next 3 weeks.

Characteristics of Dialogue

- Includes relevant, pertinent detail that supports the writer's purpose
- Makes the writing more realistic
- Makes the writing more engaging
- Is one way writers develop characters
- Uses quotation marks to enclose the exact words
- Shows a change in speaker by a change in paragraphing
- Uses phrases such as *he yelled* or *she snarled* to allow the reader to "hear" the words in the context of the situation
- Relies heavily on accurate punctuation

Supporting and Expanding Idea Development

Dialogue supports main ideas and expands thinking by the following:

- Providing a means of relating an incident
- Allowing a reader to hear what characters say about themselves or others
- Providing a glimpse into the character's personality
- Portraying the character's time period and language accurately
- Promoting understanding of the motivation of characters
- Including description of voice, expression, mannerisms, and other non-verbal means of communication
- Using short sentences and contractions to produce natural-sounding conversation
- Including fragments to illustrate a speaker's exact words or to enhance style
- Using spelling clues to indicate dialect or speech patterns

---

UNDERSTANDING THE CONCEPT OF DIALOGUE

The purpose of the learning activities in this chapter is to teach an idea development strategy for students to apply independently. When students have a clear understanding of dialogue's use for idea development, the teacher, during written or face-to-face conferencing, may suggest using this device to add depth. Students should record writing-to-learn activities from the following mini-lessons in a learning log or writer's notebook for later reference.

1. In learning logs or response journals, have students record their thinking about the following: ways to recognize that people are angry, adjectives that describe how they look or the way they might move or act, strong verbs to demonstrate their actions or movements, adverbs to describe the action, thoughts that angry people might have. Follow the same steps for other emotions (disappointed, nervous, confused, etc.).

2. Create groups of three students. Select one member of each group to be the reporter and the other two to be participants in a conversation. These conversations could be created from one of the following scenarios or one of their or your own design: a student brings home a report card with grades that are unsatisfactory; an inexperienced flyer sits in an airport waiting area while an experienced flyer nearby tries to reassure him; one person is upset about the loss of a treasured possession and a second offers assistance or comfort; one person requests from another directions for locating a local restaurant.

3. Give students a few minutes to think of what they might include in the conversation. The reporter will observe and record, from the conversation of the other two, the looks on the speakers' faces (facial expression), body movements (actions), and the way their voices sound (tone of voice).

4. Share all observations within the small group, including any thoughts the speakers may have had during the conversation.

5. As a whole class, chart responses divided into the following categories: Facial Expression, Actions, Tone of Voice, Thoughts.

- ♦ Examine the chart for similar responses in a category for the different scenarios.
- ♦ Discuss with students how similar expressions or actions can be interpreted differently depending on the situation (e.g., eyebrows drawn together could denote confusion, concern, or anger; a smile could reveal pleasure, sarcasm, or spite).

6. At this point, refer to your grammar text for a developmentally appropriate mini-lesson on the correct punctuation of dialogue.

TIPS FOR USING EXAMPLES

- ♦ Set off the speaker's exact words with quotation marks.
- ♦ Begin a new paragraph each time the speaker changes.
- ♦ Capitalize the first word of quotations.
- ♦ Place final punctuation marks inside quotation marks, in most circumstances.
- ♦ Vary the location of and word choices for the explanatory text.

7. Return to the group activity in Activity 2 (p. 78). In the same groups of three, students will use records of observations and other notes to draft a dialogue passage. They will include (as nearly as possible) words spoken, facial expressions, actions, tone of voice, and thoughts, in order to recreate the conversation for a reader. After revising dialogue passages, groups edit for punctuation and paragraphing.

UNDERSTANDING APPLICATIONS IN WRITING

1. Have students analyze the models of dialogue at the end of this chapter, samples from their grammar or literature texts, or models you have selected. Refer to the list under "Supporting and Expanding Idea Development" to note the ways writers use dialogue.

2. Assign small groups different dialogue passages from the models. Ask students to analyze how the dialogue enhances the ideas being developed and

helps to communicate the purpose to the reader. Use the following questions to guide this discussion:

- ◆ How does the dialogue passage convey the idea to the reader?
- ◆ In what ways does the dialogue make the writing realistic?
- ◆ What does the reader see, hear, feel, and think about?
- ◆ What character qualities are revealed through the dialogue?

3. Have students examine some of their recent reading (short stories, narratives, or plays) to locate passages of dialogue. In their writers' notebooks, students will analyze one or two of their located passages by referring to the list under "Supporting and Expanding Idea Development" to note the ways writers use dialogue and discuss how this support enhances the ideas being developed and communicates the purpose to the reader. They may use the questions in Activity 2 for guidance.

Mini-Lesson—Empty Dialogue

1. Share on the board or overhead the following "empty" dialogue conversation:

> "Where have you been?" she asked.
> "Out with my friends."
> "They're just using you."
> "No, they aren't."
> "You're grounded."

With a student volunteer, read aloud the dialogue above, adding no inflection, facial expression, or body language beyond cues indicated in the text. Student observers will record what they see, hear, and infer from the reading.

2. Use the following questions to assist students as they discuss their responses to the reading.

- ◆ What were the mother's reactions to her child's actions?
- ◆ What were the child's reactions to the mother?
- ◆ What can you tell about their relationship from the exchange?

If students have answers other than "I couldn't tell," to these questions, ask them to explain how the text supports their answers, as there is virtually no way to determine anything about the characters from this simplistic exchange.

Mini-Lesson—Listening to the Character

1. Put on the board or project overhead the following conversation:

"You've been with them again, haven't you?" she demanded. "How many times do I have to tell you? They don't care anything about you. They're just using you." Her voice rose to a shrill pitch.

I stammered, "But, Mom . . . "

"How do you think I feel when you're an hour late and I can't find you anywhere? " she questioned, a pleading note in her voice.

With a student volunteer, read aloud the dialogue above, adding inflection but no facial expression or body language beyond cues indicated in the text. Student observers will record what they see, hear, and infer from the reading.

2. Use the questions in Activity 2 in "Mini-Lesson—Empty Dialogue" to assist students as they discuss their responses to the reading. Students may notice that the role play reveals certain visual cues, even though none were given in the text. A person seldom speaks without some accompanying body language and facial expression. Good writers are active observers and include such cues for their readers' full participation in the text.

Mini-Lesson—Watching the Character

1. Put on the board or project overhead the following conversation:

With her hands on her hips, my mother was pacing the floor as I skulked into the kitchen. She turned, her green eyes flashing with anger and hurt. "You've been with them again, haven't you? How many times do I have to tell you? They don't care anything about you." Her pointed finger punctuated the air with every word. "They're just using you."

Shifting my weight from foot to foot, "But, Mom . . . "

"How do you think I feel when you're an hour late and I can't find you anywhere?" I wrapped my arms around her frail shoulders in a hug. Then smiled, shook my head and climbed the stairs to my room where I knew I would be for the next 3 weeks.

2. With a student volunteer, read aloud the dialogue above, adding facial expression and body language but no vocal inflection beyond cues indicated in the text. Student observers will record what they see, hear, and infer from the reading.

3. Use the questions in Activity 2 of "Mini-Lesson—Empty Dialogue" to assist students as they discuss their responses to the reading. Students may notice that the role play will reveal certain vocal cues, even though none were given in the text. Emphasize that a person seldom speaks in monotone. Because vocal expression is revealing, good writers are active listeners and include vocal cues for readers' full participation in the text.

Mini-Lesson—Thinking With the Character

1. Put on the board or project overhead the following conversation:

> One look at her face told me all I needed to know.
>   "You've been with them again, haven't you? How many times do I have to tell you? They don't care anything about you. They're just using you."
>   I tried to interject, "But, Mom . . . " However, she allowed me no opportunity for explanation.
>   "How do you think I feel when you're an hour late and I can't find you anywhere?"
>   I knew I would be exiled for the next 3 weeks.

2. With a student volunteer, read aloud only the dialogue above, adding no facial expression, body language, or vocal inflection beyond cues indicated in the text. Make sure that students have available a copy of the dialogue text to read silently the narrator's thoughts. Student observers will record what they see, hear, and infer from the reading.

3. Use the questions in Activity 2 of "Mini-Lesson—Empty Dialogue" to assist students as they discuss their responses to the reading. Students may notice that the role play will reveal certain vocal, body language, and facial expression cues, even though none were given in the text. Conversation and dialogue do not exist in a vacuum. Good writers include many types of cues for their readers' full participation in the text.

Mini-Lesson—Listening to, Watching, and Thinking With the Character

1. Put on the board or project overhead the following conversation:

> With her hands on her hips, my mother was pacing the floor as I skulked into the kitchen. One look at her face told me all I needed to know.
>   She turned, her green eyes flashing with anger and hurt. "You've been with them again, haven't you?" she demanded. "How many times do I have to tell you? They don't care anything about you." Her voice rose to a shrill pitch. "They're just using you." Her pointed finger punctuated the air with every word.
>   Shifting my weight from foot to foot, I stammered, "But, Mom . . . " However, she allowed me no opportunity for explanation.
>   "How do you think I feel when you're an hour late and I can't find you anywhere?" she questioned, a pleading note in her voice.

I wrapped my arms around her frail shoulders in a hug. Then I smiled, shook my head, and climbed the stairs to my room where I knew I would be for the next 3 weeks.

2. With a student volunteer, read aloud the complete dialogue above, adding all facial expression, body language, and vocal inflection cues indicated in the text. Make sure students have a copy of the dialogue text to read silently the narrator's thoughts. Although this is the same example used in each preceding mini-lesson, this final version models the most effective use of dialogue by including all aspects of reader involvement.

3. Students will examine the text using the following questions:

♦ What idea does the dialogue passage convey to the reader?
♦ In what ways does the dialogue make the writing realistic?
♦ What does the reader see, hear, feel, and think?
♦ What qualities of the characters are revealed through the dialogue passage?

Mini-Lesson—Creating Purposeful Dialogue

Once students have learned to write effective dialogue, they sometimes use it indiscriminately, without purpose. This mini-lesson will help students understand how to create pertinent, relevant dialogue—necessary for the reader's understanding.

1. Share the following sample of ineffectiveness. In small groups, students will refer to "Supporting and Expanding Idea Development" at the beginning of this chapter to analyze the dialogue.

> Josh and Tiffany rushed to the front of the line just in time to see the balloons in the parade pass. "Here they come," Tiffany screamed as she jumped up and down. "Here come the balloons. Look, Josh," she pointed, "there are all different kinds of animal balloons."
> "Is there an orangutan?" asked Josh, as he peered down the street. "An orangutan is a primate. I saw one at the zoo last week."
> Tiffany questioned, "Did you go to the zoo with your scout troop?"
> "No, my grandparents took me."
> "I like the monkeys best at the zoo," Tiffany said.
> "My favorites are the elephants," Josh stated.
> As the last balloon passed by the children, they turned and ran back to where their parents stood waiting to take them home.

2. Students should determine that although the dialogue is well written, the following is not relevant to the purpose:

> Tiffany questioned, "Did you go to the zoo with your scout troop?"

"No, my grandparents took me."

"I like the monkeys best at the zoo," Tiffany said.

"My favorites are the elephants," Josh stated.

Mini-Lesson—Developing Dialogue From a Prose Passage

Once students have learned to write effective dialogue, they should be encouraged to use this skill in their writing. Prose-heavy narratives, and even articles, become much more engaging to the reader when dialogue is included. This mini-lesson will call students' attention to opportunities for improving their prose with dialogue.

1. From the following, ask students to identify text that could be replaced or further developed with dialogue passages. Ask them to consider which dialogue strategies learned thus far would be most useful in each circumstance.

> Just then he heard some voices. Little Dreamer slowed his horse down and got closer to see who they were. When he saw that they were braves from the village, he rode over to greet them. They were shocked to see Little Dreamer riding a horse. Wasting no time, he told them about the soldiers and where they were camped. The braves asked no questions, just followed Little Dreamer to the camp. When they arrived, they rode into the camp yelling and swinging their weapons into the air. The soldiers were startled and ran to get their guns, but they were killed before they got them. After the attack was over, the braves realized that Little Dreamer was gone. They thought that he may be already back at the village, so they went back to find him.
>
> (4th-Grade Student)

2. Some expected student responses might include the following: *They were shocked to see Little Dreamer riding a horse* (watching the character). *Wasting no time, he told them about the soldiers and where they were camped* (listening to the character). *When they arrived, they rode into the camp yelling and swinging their weapons into the air* (watching and listening to the character). *After the attack was over, the braves realized that Little Dreamer was gone* (thinking with the character).

3. In small groups, students will rewrite the prose passage to include dialogue. Ask them to refer to the section, "Supporting and Expanding Idea Development" to make the dialogue more reader-based (meaningful, engaging, realistic). The following is one possible revision.

> Just then he heard some voices. Little Dreamer slowed his horse down and got closer to see who they were. When he saw that they were

braves from the village, he rode over to greet them. "I am pleased to see braves from my village."

"Is that our Little Dreamer on that horse?" asked the first brave incredulously.

"It cannot be! We know he is afraid to ride," announced another.

"It is I," replied Little Dreamer. "I must warn my brothers of the danger ahead. Soldiers are camped along the river that leads to our home. I fear they are preparing to attack our women and children."

The braves asked no questions, just followed Little Dreamer to the camp. When they arrived, they rode into the camp yelling and swinging their weapons into the air.

"Look at them run!" screamed Little Dreamer.

"Yes," replied the oldest brave as he pulled his horse up and laughed at the confused soldiers. "We have them on the run. Do not let them escape!"

The soldiers were startled and ran to get their guns, but they were killed before they got them.

After the attack was over, the braves prepared to return to their village. The brave who had led the attack looked around the gathering of his brothers and inquired, "Where is Little Dreamer?"

"I do not remember seeing him ride off," replied one of the braves.

Another spoke, "Perhaps he is back at the village."

4. Students will share their revisions with whole group.

APPLICATIONS TO WRITING

1. Students will revise the following ineffective dialogue, developing it into effective dialogue using the strategies of listening to the character, watching the character, and thinking with the character.

"Where's John?" asked Dennis.
"I thought he was with you," replied Mother.
"The last time I saw him, he said he would see me later," Dennis said.
"Where do you think he might be?" Mother asked.

Students may add other dialogue as well as explanatory text to create an effective passage.

2. Students will share effective dialogue passages with a partner and analyze whether the dialogue

- ◆ Sounds natural
- ◆ Gives readers a clearer understanding of characters by showing feelings, actions, thoughts, physical reactions, motivation, and so on

- ◆ Allows readers to picture the action
- ◆ Moves readers through a sequence of action toward a resolution

3. Ask students to look in their working folders and select two or three pieces in which the writing would be enhanced if they added or altered dialogue. After selecting one piece, students will make the appropriate revisions. Remind them to consider listening to the character, watching the character, thinking with the character, changing prose to dialogue, and creating purposeful dialogue.

4. With a partner, students share both the original and revised versions for feedback on the differences noted. Use the assessment checklist in "Assessing the Effective Use of Dialogue" to complete this activity.

ASSESSING THE EFFECTIVE USE OF DIALOGUE

Dialogue must:

- ❑ Be a relevant, pertinent detail that supports the writer's purpose
- ❑ Make the writing more realistic and engaging by sounding natural
- ❑ Agree with what the reader knows of the characters
- ❑ Give the reader a clearer understanding of the characters by showing feelings, actions, thoughts, physical reactions, motivation, and so on
- ❑ Allow the reader to picture the action
- ❑ Move the reader through some sequence of action toward a resolution
- ❑ Use quotation marks to enclose the exact words
- ❑ Show a change in speaker by a change in paragraphing
- ❑ Use phrases to watch the character, listen to the character, and think with the character

EXAMPLES OF DIALOGUE TO BE USED AS CLASSROOM MODELS

Students will benefit from recognizing and examining passages of dialogue as they appear in different forms of writing. The following examples are included to provide additional classroom models. To ensure that students have internalized the concept and will successfully apply it in their own writing, they must be afforded many opportunities to locate and consider the effectiveness of dialogue used for support. This need not be an added burden for the teacher, but rather should be an integral part of reading instruction that encourages students to think critically about their reading as well as their writing.

The warm fire crackles in the cool night air. An old Navajo man sits motionless by two children. "Grandfather," one of the children says, "will you tell us the story about Little Dreamer and the Sunrise?" The four bright brown eyes stare longingly at their old grandfather, anxiously awaiting his answer. (Watching the character, providing a setting)

(4th-Grade Student)

Tap, tap, tap, a knock was heard at Matt's door, "erieetch" the door creaked open.

"Why, hello, Jonathan, how are you?" greeted Matt's Mom.

"Oh, just fine; I was wondering if Matt could play?"

"Yes, I'll go get him."

This did no good for Matt had heard them talking and was swooping from the second level yelling, "Jonathan, Jonathan, look at my new compass my Uncle Joey gave me!"

"Cool, can I see it?" Jonathan said excitingly.

"Yeah but be careful it's old. Hey Mom, can we go explore at Ramhill Forest," Matt asked.

"Um . . . well, I guess so, but be back before dark," she blurted out as quickly as possible. Matt and Jonathan were already darting out the door. (Watching and listening to the character)

(4th-Grade Student)

As the crowd dwindled, Crispus began to close the covers over his supplies. Out of the corner of his eye, he notices a slim, young British soldier standing at the edge of the firelight.

"Do you have a hankering for some good brand?" Crispus called, stepping closer to the quiet young man.

"Do you have writing paper," the soldier replied. "I sure would like to write a letter back home."

Crispus opened a small compartment and pulled out a sheet of fine, white writing paper and a roll of sealing wax.

"I do," he answered. "The finest. And who will you be writing to?"

The soldier lowered himself beside the fire and answered slowly, "I am going to write for a friend of mine. He can't write himself right now."

Crispus was intrigued. "Why not?"

"Cause he's a rebel prisoner who got himself injured, that's why. Don't tell anyone," he whispered, looking around to be sure that no one was listening. "He's a fine young fella with a bad hand, and I thought I could do this one thing for him." (Watching and thinking with the character)

(7th-Grade Student)

Anyway, this same boring Saturday, Mom yelled, "John Arnold Edwards! Get down here and get this skateboard out of my living room floor! What have I told you about this skateboard?"

"You don't have to yell, Mom," I said angrily. I walked down the hall, entered the living room, and what did I see? Mom was wearing a plaid shirt with checkered pants! "Mom!" I said, "What do you have on?"

"Oh, I just thought I'd try something new. You like it?" Mom asked.

"Oh . . . um . . . it's nice," I lied. (Always lie to your mom about her appearance.)

Then my fifteen-year-old sister walked through the door wearing a black leather skirt and a Joe Boxer shirt with some big, old-fashioned shoes. "Mom!" my sister said. "Nice outfit, welcome to the 90's."

Now her name is Samantha, but we call her Sam, for short. She thinks she is all that and a bag of potato chips, too. (Watching, listening to, and thinking with the character)

(7th-Grade Student)

She thought the world of Haze and loved everything about him. She loved his devotion to the farm, his devotion to tradition, and his devotion to being a good man. She loved Haze because he was simply intelligent.

"Oh, my dear wife, of course I know when you walk in a room!" he said in an amused tone. "I know the way you smell better than I know the way I smell."

She looked at Hazel with a kindred expression, as if this were something that she had heard before but would be happy to hear over and over again for the rest of her life.

"I brought you some coffee," she said as she handed it to him with both arms outstretched.

"Thanks, Hon, I was getting a bit chilly out here all alone. Doesn't this new crop look nice? It'll be the first of the season, ready to go by the beginning of March."

"Yes, yes, yes, it's lovely," she said in a tone that proved that sod was a passion that she and Hazel did not share. "I'm going back to the house. I got a lot of dresses to work on."

Hazel watched Clarity float through the aisles and out the door before he turned to watch the empty driveway. (Listening to, watching, thinking with the character)

(12th-Grade Student)

The doctor threw down his notepad. "That's it! This kid is too crazy for me," he murmured, and then added aloud, "Josh, you didn't see anything! There were no soldiers coming out of any wall! Don't you get that?"

Josh grew pale. "I saw them; I swear," he said weakly. "I really did. I'm NOT CRAZY!" he screamed as he grabbed a paperweight off the table and hurled it against the wall. "You can cut open my head and see for yourself! I saw those SOLDIERS. I did!"

The doctor pushed a button on his desk, then attempted to calm Josh. Josh flailed his arms and backed away. His long hair fell in his face, hiding tears of frustration.

"Now, Josh," the doctor was cooing. "Be good—"

Josh pushed himself into the corner. "Don't touch me!" he wailed, facing the wall. "You think I'm crazy, and I'm NOT." (Listening to and watching the character)

(12th-Grade Student)

CHAPTER SUMMARY

When used effectively, dialogue is one of the most useful tools a writer has to successfully communicate with an audience. However, most inexperienced writers lack the subtlety necessary to use this idea development strategy to provide the reader with relative, pertinent information.

The various dialogue skills addressed in this chapter will assist writers as they develop ideas through purposeful conversation and explanatory text. In a standards-based curriculum, students learn to read and write personal expressive, literary, and expository text. This chapter offers teaching suggestions designed to enhance student learning in these genres.

8   Anecdotes

As a young teacher, I learned the hard way the peril of leaving my class unattended. Returning from the principal's office one busy day, I found the door to my classroom locked with my class inside. "Let me in, you guys," I said as I pulled on the doorknob.

When no one came to the door, I stood on tiptoe to look through the tiny door pane. With their backs to the door, my entire class ignored my pleading. The room's side windows were open, though, so I headed outside to climb through the window in order to regain control of my class.

Balancing myself on the window's ledge, I climbed through a window that pulled open into the room. This was not a simple task; but I did it, dragging in one leg at a time. I turned to push the window closed, then moved to face the class. Instead, my eyes met those of the district superintendent just entering the door.

Anecdotes, little stories such as the one above, are used to engage and entertain audiences of all kinds. Anecdotes occur naturally in speaking. Good speakers often hold the attention of their audiences when they share anecdotes related to their topic. Writers, too, use the anecdote to elicit responses from readers. In many cases, the use of the anecdote causes a reader to pause and reflect on a kindred experience. We all have our "little stories," and their similarities and differences make communication a more enjoyable and stimulating activity. Anecdotes add flavor to the connection writers establish with their audience. They evoke a smile, a grimace, a compassionate nod, or an empathetic personal response.

The anecdote itself may become the explanation for a situation or provide insight into a character's motivation or personality, as it allows readers to draw their own conclusions. For example, in the anecdote above, one might conclude that the teacher involved was either derelict of duty or the victim of a practical joke. In either case, the audience is left wondering what, if any, repercussions resulted. This anecdote allows the writer or speaker to make a point about inexperience while softening and humanizing the text.

A series of anecdotes may establish the validity of a point the writer is making by adding layers of evidence. To provide connections to events over time, an anecdotal series leads a reader through events toward a logical conclusion. A writer's purpose becomes more personal when the reader understands by "seeing" through such a series.

Student writing may begin to "come alive" when students feel free to make connections to readers in personal ways through anecdotes. The writing teacher who sees the need to arm students with as many successful writing strategies as possible can do so by teaching the use of anecdotes.

TEACHING STUDENTS TO USE ANECDOTES

An anecdote is a brief narration of an event.

Example

In response to the question concerning how long a man's legs should be, Abraham Lincoln responded, "After much thought and consideration, not to mention mental worry and anxiety, it is my opinion, all side issues being swept aside, that a man's lower limbs, in order to preserve harmony of proportion, should be at least long enough to reach from his body to the ground."

Characteristics of Anecdotes

- Are brief
- Engage the reader
- Recount highlights of an event concisely
- Allow the reader to experience the scene
- Support the writer's purpose
- Are interesting, amusing, or dramatic
- Are often written from the first-person point of view

Supporting and Expanding Idea Development

Anecdotes support main ideas and expand thinking by

- Illustrating a point for the reader
- Clarifying a point for the reader
- Providing the reader with a concrete image
- Creating connections to the reader's own experiences
- Revealing something about the writer (in some instances)

UNDERSTANDING THE USE OF ANECDOTES

The purpose of the learning activities in this chapter is to teach an idea development strategy for students to apply independently. When students have a clear understanding of the use of anecdotes for idea development, the teacher, during written or face-to-face conferencing, may suggest using this device to add depth. Students should record writing-to-learn activities from the following mini-lessons in a writer's notebook for later reference.

1. Direct students to record lists or sketches of amusing, dramatic, or unusual occurrences. These responses should be compiled in their writer's notebook, learning log, or journal. Ask students to choose an incident to tell to a partner. They should choose one that can be related in 2 minutes or less.

2. Use the following questions for students to respond to each other's "verbal anecdotes."

- What, specifically, did you find engaging about the account?
- What parts created a visual image for you?
- Does this account remind you of a similar experience of your own? If so, share it with your partner.

3. Share with students the following excerpt and have them examine the italicized anecdote. Use the characteristics of anecdotes listed earlier to further define this idea development strategy if necessary.

> Zarmo, the comedy tramp juggler, was a disciplinarian who practiced his juggling for hours every morning as soon as the theatre opened. We could see him backstage balancing a billiard cue on his chin and throwing a billiard ball up and catching it on the tip of the cue, then throwing up another and catching that on top of the first ball—which

he often missed. For four years, he told Mr. Jackson, he had been practicing that trick and at the end of the week he intended to try it out for
the first time with the audience. *That night we all stood in the wings
and watched him. He did it perfectly—and the first time!—throwing
the ball up and catching that on top of the first. But the audience only
applauded mildly. Mr. Jackson often told the story of that night. Said he
to Zarmo, "You make the trick look to easy, you don't sell it. You
should miss it several times, then do it." Zarmo laughed, "I am not
expert enough to miss it yet."*

(Weiss, 1970, p. 36)

4. Ask students to read the excerpt without the anecdote (italics) and discuss
the difference in the text for the reader. Then ask students to read only the anecdote. Discuss how, without a context, the anecdote is not a useful writing strategy.

UNDERSTANDING
APPLICATIONS IN WRITING

1. Have students analyze models of anecdotes (see "Examples of Anecdotes to
Be Used As Classroom Models" at the end of the chapter). In selected models,
students will identify the characteristics of anecdotes. Discuss how this form of
support enhances the idea(s) being developed and helps to communicate the
purpose of the piece to the reader.

2. Have students read from a variety of sources to recognize and select anecdotes. Examples are readily accessible in newspapers and magazines such as
Reader's Digest, Highlights, Scholastic Scope and many others. Passages containing
anecdotes may be copied and anecdotes highlighted by students to be examined
for understanding.

3. Students will read and examine the student-selected anecdotes and discuss
how they enhance the writer's purpose for readers (see "Supporting and Expanding Idea Development" at the beginning of this chapter).

4. The following questions are designed to assist students in their analysis of
student-selected anecdotes:

♦ How does the writer introduce the anecdote?
♦ What point is the writer trying to make by using this anecdote?
♦ How does this anecdote add to the writer's point?
♦ What experiences does this anecdote make you remember?
♦ How does this anecdote make the writing more interesting?
♦ How does this anecdote clarify the writer's purpose?

♦ How does the writer employ the following to help the reader to experience the scene: "showing" sentences and language; sensory details; precise nouns, verbs, adjectives, and adverbs; subjective description—similes, metaphors?

5. Put on the board or project overhead the following incident: *It was funny the time my spaghetti landed in Mrs. Smith's hair.* Have students generate questions they need answered to understand what actually took place. If students have difficulty beginning, you might wish to offer some of the following:

♦ Where did this happen? (In the school cafeteria)
♦ When did this happen? (As I walked into the cafeteria to sit with my friends)
♦ Who is Mrs. Smith? (The 4th-grade teacher)
♦ How exactly did this happen? (There were kernels of corn on the floor, and I slipped on them. The tray went flying into the air and landed on Mrs. Smith.)
♦ How did Mrs. Smith react? (She got up from her seat. I thought she would be mad, but she just laughed.)

6. Use the answers to these questions to model how this information enhances idea development within the anecdote. If the above answers were used, the anecdote developed might be similar to the following.

> Even teachers have a sense of humor. One day when we had spaghetti for lunch, the cafeteria lady filled my plate full with the gooey mixture. As I walked into the cafeteria to sit with my friends, I slipped on some kernels of yellow corn. My body contorted to avoid a fall, sending the tray flying into the air. When I looked up, there sat the 4th-grade teacher, Mrs. Smith, with greasy pasta strings cascading from her hair. Slowly she rose from her seat, turned toward me, and began to laugh.

If student-generated answers were used, the example should reflect the answers generated by the class to the questions in Activity 5. If you wish to teach students how to analyze an anecdote, have them analyze the above sample or one generated by the class.

APPLICATIONS TO WRITING

1. Direct students to return to the beginning activity in their writer's notebook or think of another time when something was particularly funny, silly, sad, painful, confusing, weird, or embarrassing. Once they have decided on one such memory, students will recall and mentally reenact an incident that an audience might find engaging. They will then share the incident aloud with a partner, concentrating on "showing" the action rather than "telling." (See the chapter on description for a clear definition of these terms.)

2. The partner will ask questions to clarify the incident for the audience, addressing the elements of who, what, when, where, why, and how. After both partners share, students will draft their anecdotes.

3. Students will exchange drafts with the same partner and offer suggestions to make the anecdote meet the criteria of an effective anecdote. If necessary, instruct students to refer to the list of characteristics of anecdotes at the beginning of this chapter.

4. Students will revise the anecdote based on the input provided by peers and exchange drafts with their partner for any further suggestions or input. After a second revision, the teacher will examine the product and respond appropriately for further revision or with reteaching.

5. Students will analyze their revised anecdote to determine in what type of writing this anecdote would help develop an idea for readers. Refer to models read earlier and classroom readings. For example, students may see an anecdote as most effectively supporting a feature article about kindness to others; a how-to article about creating an African art mask; a commentary discussing spelling rules; or a memoir about a grandmother's unusual, but endearing, habits. Discuss writing situations where this anecdote would enhance idea development.

6. Provide adequate time for students to return to their working folders to reexamine previously drafted pieces, looking for places where an anecdote used as support would add depth or audience awareness. Students will make the appropriate revisions to previous drafts.

OTHER SUGGESTIONS FOR CRAFTING ANECDOTES

For students who still require focused practice on effectively developing anecdotes, the following suggestions may be useful. For students who have internalized this skill, the suggestions may be used as enrichment activities.

1. Have students think of a time when someone was rude to them, they were injured, something funny happened to them, they had a great deal of fun doing something, or they were embarrassed. Explain the circumstances around it.

2. Encourage students to search their writings for just such general statements and develop these insignificant generalities into audience-engaging anecdotes.

3. Use action pictures from magazines, yearbooks, and newspapers to create scenarios for which an anecdote might be written.

4. Use the lead-in statements from other identified anecdotes to create a differ-ent anecdotal possibility for the speaker or writer.

5. Ask the class make some general statements about the school; for example, "The hallways of our school are crowded" or "The parking lot is like a demolition derby." After creating a list of statements, students will select one and develop it into a paragraph using an anecdote as the main form of development. This activity will also assist students with learning to write effective paragraphs. The teacher may create other engaging activities for additional student learning and enrichment.

ASSESSING THE EFFECTIVE USE OF ANECDOTES

As teachers or peers assess the application of anecdotes in student writing, the following criteria should be addressed.

An anecdote must:

❑ Support the focused purpose of the writing and main idea of the paragraph
❑ Allow the reader to experience the scene through the following: "showing" sentences and language; sensory details; precise nouns, pronouns, verbs, ad-jectives, and adverbs; subjective description (similes, metaphors, etc.)
❑ Engage the reader through concise highlights of the event
❑ Briefly illustrate a point for the reader

The anecdote may:

❑ Create a connection from the writing to the reader's own experiences
❑ Reveal something about the writer

EXAMPLES OF ANECDOTES TO BE USED AS CLASSROOM MODELS

Students will benefit from recognizing and examining anecdotes as they appear in different forms of writing. The following examples are included to provide addi-tional classroom models. To ensure that students have internalized the concept and will successfully apply it in their own writing, they must be afforded many oppor-tunities to locate and consider the effectiveness of anecdotes used for support. This need not be an added burden for the teacher, but rather should be an integral part of reading instruction that encourages students to think critically about their read-ing as well as their writing. The anecdotes in each of the following samples are denoted by italics.

When I was three, I had a book called My Little Dinosaur. *It was about a boy who found a live dinosaur in a cave near his house. I started wanting a dinosaur, too.*

My dad worked with dinosaurs at a museum — so I asked him to get me one. "Christmas would be a good time," I told him. Of course, Dad couldn't really bring me a dinosaur. And as I grew up, I forgot about wanting one.

(Rich & Menzel, 1995, p. 33)

Frank O'Connor, the Irish writer, tells in one of his books how as a boy, he and his friends would make their way across the countryside and when they came to an orchard wall that seemed too high and too doubtful to try and too difficult to permit their voyage to continue, they took off their hats and tossed them over the wall — and then they had no choice but to follow them. This Nation has tossed its cap over the wall of space, and we have no choice but to follow it. Whatever the difficulties, they will be overcome.

(Kennedy, 1963)

In my sensory education I include my physical awareness of the word. Of a certain word, that is, the connection it has with what it stands for. *At around age six, perhaps, I was standing by myself in our front yard waiting for supper, just at that hour in a late summer day when the sun is already below the horizon and the risen full moon in the visible sky stops being chalky and begins to take on light. There comes the moment, and I saw it then, when the moon goes from flat to round. For the first time it met my eyes as a globe. The word "moon" came into my mouth as though fed to me out of a silver spoon. Held in my mouth the moon became a word. It had the roundness of a Concord grape Grandpa took off his vine and gave me to suck out of its skin and swallow whole, in Ohio.*

(Welty, 1995, p. 61)

I'm from South Korea and I'm an American citizen. Even though Koreans are not black, every one of us that I know has been discriminated against. I have been laughed at for my race and my style of clothes. Some people even call me Chinese eyes, Japanese girl, Chinese girl, or Asian girl. *One day when I was selling candy bars, a boy answered the door and yelled to his mom, "Mom, there's a Chinese girl selling candy bars!"* After he said this, I felt insulted. Whenever I get laughed at I feel like crying.

(4th-Grade Student)

Seeing Jennifer was usually forbidden, because she was older and a "bad influence." But that never stopped me. *One summer my oldest sister was having a slumber party with six of her friends. I had Jennifer over and while the girls were downstairs, we raided their bags. We poured Sea Breeze in them, exchanged clothes with other bags and squirted toothpaste in them. The burning wrath of my father came down hard—not literally, but definitely figuratively.*

(8th-Grade Student)

At recess one Friday, two of my musically inclined friends and I were sitting [on the school playground], and practicing the assigned pieces on our plastic recorders. I was perfectly content with "Hot Cross Buns" until I realized that something was dreadfully wrong . . . Where were the boys? . . . my eyes [began] sweeping the playground for the miscreants. I finally located a group of them, standing in a loose knot in the shade of one of our playground's old oak trees. The boys were stomping at the tree's base, laughing insanely and shouting something unintelligible. If I had been more interested in William Golding than in Laura Ingalls Wilder at the time, I probably would not have been surprised to discover that they were chanting, "Kill the pig!"

(12th-Grade Student)

One day, during gym class—as I waited until last to be picked for a team—I noticed something among the rows of girls and boys. It was something I had never paid much attention to before. I really was quite unique compared to those popular girls, and I began to see why. To be sure that I was right, I compared myself to Sue Blue, the most popular girl in my school. As I looked from her to me, I thought to myself:

"O.K. . . . makeup . . . now me . . . no makeup . . . tried that! Humm . . . fixed hair," I twisted my poker straight hair in my fingers. "Nope, no curls here . . . Shaved smooth legs . . ." I looked down at my kiwis and blushed. "O.K. . . . bra . . . Wait just a second . . ." I looked down myself and could easily see my belly and my toes . . . My little mosquito bites held up just fine on their own, thank you. "No wonder the boys pay no attention to me. I look just like them!"

(12th-Grade Student)

CHAPTER SUMMARY

To develop writing that meets local, state, and national writing standards, students must learn how to develop ideas through strategies such as the anecdote. Anecdotes are frequently found in lead-ins to articles or used to develop ideas in memoirs and speeches.

Anecdotes can help writers communicate their ideas to an audience by eliminating unsupported generalities, oversimplification, circular thinking, unsubstantiated opinions, and repetition.

By their very nature, anecdotes provide specific development of an idea and provoke a response from a reader. Anecdotes appear in all successful forms of communication, and student writing will be more effective when students learn the appropriate use of this strategy to develop ideas.

9 ◆ Vignettes

Through the eye of a camera, the photographer captures moments in time to be saved for posterity. Writers, too, capture moments for an audience. Their pens may lead readers into battle, transport them across space and time, or trigger the recall in the mind's eye of some scene or event. The vignette is a writer's photograph. Through it, writers add dimension to readers' understanding.

The word *precision* is often used to describe the vignette as a support element. Although all writing requires decision making by the writer, the vignette requires a subtlety and delicacy not typically applied. When a writer crafts a vignette, he or she creates an indelible image to enhance the reader's perception of an idea.

The vignette will of necessity be brief; therefore this concise narrative or sketch is not a development strategy to be used in every form of writing. This selective use of the vignette requires a careful analysis of purpose and audience. "Moments" chosen for elaboration by a vignette must be significant to the purpose, as it provides a vivid picture of a scene by creating an image with words. The language decisions made regarding those "moments" become paramount. Writers do not use two words when one will suffice. Precisely chosen nouns and verbs develop images quickly and powerfully for the reader.

This necessary precision often causes writers the most difficulty. Inexperienced writers frequently concentrate on seeing through the lens rather than on developing the picture. Their "telling" rushes readers through a scene or event, without allowing them to experience it. When a vignette is used effectively, readers perceive a sharply focused image. Behind the closed eye, this image is imprinted and becomes for readers a visual connection to the text.

The vignette serves a variety of literary purposes. Occasionally, it is developed as a separate entity and treated as a distinct genre of writing. As an idea development technique, however, it depends on the context of the writing to give it meaning.

Whether it provides the lead-in for an article, a reader connection for a narrative, a setting for a short story, or the stimulus for reader reflection, the vignette can be one of a writer's most powerful tools.

TEACHING STUDENTS TO USE VIGNETTES

A vignette is a brief narrative or sketch, written with precision, intended to provide a vivid picture of a scene by creating an image with words.

Example

> Ripples run across the surface of the water. A moss-covered adult and baby manatee are going for a swim, twirling around and around slowly in the cool Gulf waters. Colorful fish pass side-by-side as the manatee's mighty flippers stroke the water with very little force. A moving object appears on the surface, a boat with a sharp, twirling propeller, just missing them by an inch.
>
> (4th Grade Student)

Characteristics of the Vignette

- Is brief
- Transports the reader into the event
- Captures a moment in time rather than telling a complete story
- Creates an image with words
- Is written, in most cases, in the present tense
- Is sometimes revealed through dialogue or careful description
- Does not rely on writer's interpretive comments or explanations

---

Supporting and Expanding Idea Development

Vignettes support main ideas and expand thinking by

- Illustrating a point for the reader
- Clarifying a point for the reader
- Providing a concrete image, showing rather than telling
- Allowing the reader to experience the scene vicariously
- Providing the reader with insight through an intense portrayal
- Providing, through a series, support for an extended narrative's purpose (as in a personal essay or memoir)

UNDERSTANDING THE USE OF VIGNETTES

The purpose of the learning activities in this chapter is to teach an idea development strategy for students to apply independently. When students have a clear understanding of the uses of the vignette as support for idea development, the teacher, during written or face-to-face conferencing, may suggest using this device to add depth. Students should record writing-to-learn activities from the following mini-lessons in a learning log or writer's notebook.

1. Direct students to examine the models of vignettes located at the end of this chapter. In these models, students will identify characteristics of the vignette by using the "Characteristics of the Vignette" section of this chapter. After analysis, discuss how this support enhances ideas being developed and helps to communicate the purpose of a piece to the reader.

2. Have students read from a variety of sources to recognize and select vignettes. Examples of readily accessible sources are newspapers and magazines such as *Reader's Digest, Highlights,* and *Scholastic Scope.* Passages containing vignettes may be copied and vignettes highlighted by students to examine in groups or to post in the room.

3. Read and examine student-selected vignettes and discuss how they enhance the writer's purpose for readers. Students may refer to the "Supporting and Expanding Idea Development" section of this chapter to identify the specificity of the vignettes' support.

Mini-Lesson—Analyzing Vignettes

1. As students begin the task of analyzing vignettes for their effective use in writing, they will require practice to fully develop the skill of analysis. Until students can analyze the vignettes they identify in their reading, they will be unsuccessful in developing their own. The following example is useful in introducing the skill of analysis.

> I was shaking in my boots as I jammed my foot into the skates. My sweaty fingers kept dropping the shoelaces as I was fastening the 10-pound weights to my feet. My ankles pounded as the skates were tightly fastened. I could feel them giving me blisters. I about fell as I

awkwardly stood up. I waddled like a penguin across the room to enter the crowded rink. I hope I don't fall in front of everybody.

(4th-Grade Student)

Use the following questions to analyze the vignette above and then apply this analysis to other teacher-generated and student-generated examples. Some suggested responses are provided.

♦ What concrete image is depicted through the vignette? How does it *show*, not *tell*? (The reader understands the writer's anxiety as he or she puts on the skates and enters the rink. The writer makes readers feel as if they are putting on the skates and entering the rink.)

♦ What language (specific nouns, vigorous verbs, etc.) creates this concrete image? (*Shaking, jammed, sweaty, dropping shoelaces, fastening 10-pound weights, ankles pounding, blisters, awkwardly, waddled, crowded rink*)

♦ How do sentence variety and length communicate the image? Note that the developmental level of the 4th-grade writer is responsible for the limited sentence variety. (Longer sentences move readers through the process of putting on the skates and entering the rink. The more simplistic sentence in form of the writer's thoughts brings readers back to the writer's perspective of the event.)

♦ How does this vignette make the writing more interesting? (It engages readers by transporting them to the setting and into the event.)

♦ What does this vignette add to the point the writer is trying to make? (It magnifies the significance of the anxiety the writer experienced about skating for the first time.)

♦ What insight does the vignette provide for readers? (Without actually "saying" that he or she is anxious about this situation, the writer clearly conveys the emotional impact of the event.)

♦ How does this vignette clarify readers' understanding of the writer's purpose? (It clarifies readers' interpretation of the writer's first adventure in ice skating as one that will not be easily forgotten.)

2. Discuss the variety of locations in which the vignettes are found in the previous student-selected complete text examples. Use the following questions to help students see the deliberate placement of vignettes as writers attempt to engage their audiences.

♦ Where in the piece was the vignette located?
♦ What idea does this vignette support or develop?
♦ How would your perception of the piece be changed if the vignette were removed?

- ◆ Would this vignette be as effective if located somewhere else in the piece of writing? Explain your response.

UNDERSTANDING APPLICATIONS IN WRITING

1. Share on the board or an overhead transparency the following sentence: *Bonnie Blair is the fastest woman on ice.* Have students generate the questions they need answered to see the action reported in the sentence. If students have difficulty beginning, you might ask questions regarding where the event happened; how the action could be shown; whether Bonnie Blair can skate.

2. The vignette below illustrates how a writer used answers to questions such as those above to enhance idea development and support the purpose. It should be obvious that the creation of a vignette to develop a specific idea or elaborate a fact, such as Bonnie Blair is the fastest woman on ice, creates an image in the reader's mind that moves far beyond the immediate fact.

> The crowd in Hamar, Norway, *rises to its feet* as Bonnie Blair zooms around the *skating oval* at 35 miles per hour. Her *powerful* legs *stroke* left and right, *propelling* her forward. *Bent at the waist,* her arms *pumping wildly,* she *glides* into the *final stretch* of the 1000-meter race. With a *final push* across the finish line, Bonnie has it again. The world's fastest woman has earned her fifth gold medal and become the most successful female Olympian of all time.
>
> (Kaminsky, 1995, p. 10)

Point out to students that the image created through the vignette results from the specificity of language choice and usage, not just from adding modifiers to nouns and verbs. To reinforce students' analysis skills, have them analyze the above sample using the questions in "Mini-Lesson—Analyzing Vignettes," Activity 2.

3. To check for understanding, use the sentence in Activity 1 of this section and ask students (in small groups) to compose a vignette of their own about Bonnie Blair and compare it to Kaminsky's. Students should not have access to Kaminsky's vignette while composing their own.

APPLICATIONS TO WRITING

1. Provide photographs from magazines or other sources and ask students to choose one photo for a writer's notebook activity. Instruct them to jot down lists or clusters or images from the photo (words or phrases only). For example, students

might be viewing a photo of a manatee and her baby swimming in the ocean. Many different-colored fish surround them and there is a boat near them in the water. The following information may be included in a response to the manatee picture: manatee and baby manatee swimming; a boat speeding through the blue gulf water; ripples on the water's surface and around the manatee and baby; different-colored fish swimming beneath the water's surface. Share with students the example provided at the beginning of this chapter as a vignette that might have been developed from this list of information.

2. Each student will then return to his or her own photo list and draft a vignette. Remind students that vignettes do not exist in isolation. As students share their vignette drafts, discuss the possibilities for a larger piece of writing for which their vignette could be used as support for a larger idea.

3. Ask students to locate in their working folders some works-in-progress that contain "telling" rather than "showing" sentences. Pass around an overhead transparency or use chart paper or sentence strips for students to record and share "telling" sentences. Students will choose one of the "telling" sentences (their own or that of another student) to replace with a vignette. Students will generate and answer questions to elaborate on the chosen sentence to create for the reader an image with words. It is important that students consider what they want their writing to do and how their reader might respond. Students will then revise the sentence by creating a vignette to take its place.

4. With a partner, each student will share the original sentence he or she selected and the vignette created to replace it. The following questions can be used to assist in analyzing the effectiveness of the newly created vignette.

- What did the vignette provide for you that the sentence did not?
- What feelings, thoughts, or emotions did you experience?
- What sensory or physical details were included?
- What image was created for you?
- What else do you need to know to better interpret the scene?

Students will then determine a type of writing in which the vignette would help develop an idea for the reader. For example, students may see a vignette as most effectively introducing a feature article; supporting a personal narrative, memoir, or essay; developing the important action or the setting in a short story; or beginning a commentary (personalized editorial).

5. Provide time for students to return to their working folders to reexamine previously drafted pieces and include vignette support to add depth or audience awareness. Students will make the appropriate revisions. This would be an effective writing-to-learn activity for students to place in a learning log, writer's

notebook, or working folder. Some students may want to develop an entire piece of writing around this particular vignette, whereas others may wish to include it as a supporting detail in a later piece of writing. Others may wish to do nothing further with the writing.

ASSESSING THE EFFECTIVE USE OF VIGNETTES

Vignettes must:

- ❑ Support the focused purpose of the writing and the main idea of the paragraph
- ❑ Be brief
- ❑ Capture just a moment in time
- ❑ Create a concrete image with words
- ❑ Stand on their own without interpretive comments or explanations
- ❑ Transport the reader into the event through the intensity of the portrayal

Vignettes may:

- ❑ Be written in present tense
- ❑ Contain dialogue with descriptive explanatory text
- ❑ Provide a lead-in (hook) for a piece of writing
- ❑ Provide support for an extended narrative's purpose

EXAMPLES OF VIGNETTES TO BE USED AS CLASSROOM MODELS

Students will benefit from recognizing and examining vignettes as they appear in different forms of writing. The following examples are included to provide additional classroom models. To ensure that students have internalized the concept and will successfully apply it in their own writing, they must be afforded many opportunities to locate and consider the effectiveness of vignettes used for support. This need not be an added burden for the teacher, but rather should be an integral part of reading instruction that encourages students to think critically about their reading as well as their writing. Vignettes in each of the following samples are denoted by italics.

> *A shallow fly ball sailed over the shortstop's head. Pivoting, center fielder Shanti "Vince" Beal streaked to intercept it, craning his head over his shoulder to keep the falling ball in view. Then, in one flowing*

sequence, the lean six-footer seemed to will the ball right into his out-stretched glove.

(Dimmitt, 1997, p. 128)

The view is awesome. *Though the sky above is overcast, you can see treetops in the valley below as you climb to the summit of a 3,600-meter peak. Suddenly the wind starts to howl. Within minutes, you're caught in a blizzard, unable to see. Huddling against the rocky cliff, you bury your face in your parka . . .*

("Cliffhanger," 1994, pp. 18-19)

I was shaking in my boots as I jammed my foot into the skates. My sweaty fingers kept dropping the shoelaces as I was fastening the 10-pound weights to my feet. My ankles pounded as the skates were tightly fastened. I could feel them giving me blisters. I about fell as I awkwardly stood up. I waddled like a penguin across the room to enter the crowded rink. I hope I don't fall in front of everybody.

(4th-Grade Student)

I knew something was very wrong. I turned my head to see the top of a pick-up truck nearing. I began screaming hysterically. The glistening ice ripped at the runners on the sled. I was going faster and faster. My eyes blurred and everything was in a whirlwind. I saw trees speeding past me. Jody was nervously gripping her head, screaming. I felt chilled, not only by the ice, but by the fact that I was going to be hit by a truck. I dragged my fingers along the ice, frantically trying to stop myself. Everything seemed so loud, overpowering, and deafening. I saw the truck's wheel, heard the horn, felt the ice, and leaned over in a last attempt to save myself.

At the last moment, I shut my eyes, waiting for the madness to end . . .

(7th-Grade Student)

Either she finally picked up on the messages I had been furiously sending her, or she finally got around to grading them. Mrs. Brown grabbed our writing assignments, adjusted her bifocal, square, reading glasses to sit precisely on the bridge of her nose, licked the business end of her red grading pencil, and began reading. At that point I began to writhe painfully in my desk.

(12th-Grade Student)

Of the many papers I've cranked out at crunch time, my midnight bat-tle with Macbeth *and* Shakespeare *is the most memorable. At twelve o'clock on the night before the due date of my literary essay, I was sprawled across my bed glaring with teary eyes at my weak and unclear analysis paper. Surrounded by broken pencils and several shredded drafts, I hurled my over-stuffed English folder and my copy of* Macbeth *against my bedroom door and erupted into loud curses and pathetic sobs.*

(12th-Grade Student)

CHAPTER SUMMARY

By creating for the reader indelible images and precise connections to the purpose of the piece, the vignette is a powerful communication skill, but one that is difficult to master. Since vignettes do not exist in isolation, in this chapter students are taught to create vignettes that further develop ideas.

Writers should understand that vignettes are not appropriate idea development strategies for all types of writing and should be used selectively and sparingly.

Analysis

10

When we analyze, we are really asking many questions: What's going on here? What's it all about? How did this occur? Why did it occur? Who's involved? What's involved? We are interested in examining the parts that make up the issue, situation, or problem. Our analysis will lead us back to consideration of the whole once more, its overall meaning or function.

(Betthauser, 1995, p. 160)

Analysis as an idea development strategy is both crucial to excellent writing and difficult to teach. It is crucial to excellent writing because it elicits abstract thinking from a reader; it is difficult to teach because of the inherent abstraction. Analysis depends on critical-thinking skills developed over time through reading, writing, and other content practices. No worksheet can teach a student to analyze. Therefore increasing students' abilities to develop ideas that reflect analysis of thought is an ongoing instructive process in every classroom.

Successful analysis depends on both the writer's ability to provide thinking opportunities and the reader's reflective connections to the thinking. When writing invites a reader to think beyond the words on the page and make reflective connections, the writer's communication of his or her ideas has been successful. Although reflection is indeed analysis, it requires a more personal, emotional commitment from the writer. Reflective details and statements in a piece of writing provide a means for the writer to comment on the present, the past, or the future. Reflection personalizes writing because it allows the reader to understand the importance of the subject to the writer. As an idea development strategy, reflection provides a window into the writer's mind.

Effective writers use analysis and reflection to craft words that compel readers to make reflective connections. Most student writing at any grade level contains generalities and unsophisticated development of ideas. Even when a student learns and begins to employ strategies such as cause and effect or comparison and contrast, the writing may lack the necessary specificity, which comes from a thinking analysis of ideas to be shared with a reader.

Writers who understand the complementary relationship of reading and writing recognize situations that lend themselves to analysis and reflective development while creating opportunities for reflective connections and insight. By experiencing reflective connections as a reader, a writer learns to craft words that promote analysis.

Simply teaching activities that promote analysis and reflection will not ensure that students will be able to use this critical-thinking skill effectively in their reading and writing. Students will require more rehearsals in various reading and writing instruction to develop confidence and proficiency. For student success, teachers must provide instructional direction in the form of immediate, specific response.

TEACHING STUDENTS TO USE ANALYSIS

Analysis is a basic human reasoning process that requires the critical examination of ideas, information, and thinking. Reflective analysis establishes the writer's personal reaction. Through analysis, each part of a larger whole is explained separately and related to the whole. Through reflective analysis, the writer's point of view is evident.

Characteristics of Analysis

- Supports the writer's purpose
- Engages and involves the reader
- Shows the relationships of the parts to one another and to the whole
- Relates ideas to other ideas, content, or personal connections
- Interprets information

> ### Supporting and Expanding Idea Development
>
> Analysis supports main ideas and expands thinking by
>
> - Providing thought-provoking connections for the reader
> - Allowing the reader to understand patterns, relationships, connections, or personal reactions
> - Providing the reader with precise thought and logic
> - Allowing the reader to examine information or experiences
> - Establishing and developing cause-and-effect relationships
> - Providing an expansion of the facts and information in the writing

UNDERSTANDING THE CONCEPT OF ANALYSIS

The learning activities in this chapter are designed to teach an idea development strategy for students to apply independently. When students can analyze the ideas necessary to communicate with an audience, the teacher, during written or face-to-face conferencing, may specifically suggest strategies to enhance the elaboration and understanding for particular audiences. Students should record writing-to-learn activities from the following mini-lessons in a learning log or writer's notebook for later reference.

1. Consider large topics or concepts related to classroom instruction, for example: mammals, friendship, cultures, democratic principles, or scientific theories. Instruct students to brainstorm as many subtopics of the selected topic or concept they can think of. For example, if the topic of mammals is chosen, the brainstorming might come up with *bear, cow, dog, pig, horse, coyote, wolf, deer, dolphin, hamster, whale, bobcat, bat, buffalo, cat,* or *fox.* Students should then categorize the brainstormed list, looking for commonalties among the subtopics. This categorizing may be similar to the following: *Pets—dog, cat, hamster; Ocean—whale, dolphin; Wild—bear, buffalo, bobcat, coyote, wolf, fox.*

Select one response as a topic to be explored and brainstorm possible subtopics. For example, if the topic chosen is wolf, subtopics might include *habitat, gestation period, litter size, caring for young, population, appearance, feeding, predator versus prey,* and *life span.* Depending on the topic or concept being analyzed, the analysis may be more specific. Additionally, any brainstormed list could be analyzed and divided into a variety of categories.

2. Students will then select one subtopic and brainstorm all information either previously known or researched about this subtopic. For example, if the subtopic *caring for the young* is selected, the brainstormed possibilities might include the following: *Mothers dig the den to give birth; newborns are not allowed to venture out of the den; older members of the pack hunt and kill food; parents and older members of the pack participate in play with the young.*

Students will take the information gathered and develop each of these final subtopics through analysis to communicate the subtopic to readers. The analysis of information is best supported when writers provide reasons (whys or hows) for their statements (whats). The following example demonstrates one manner in which the idea of caring for young wolves may be developed. Ask students to identify the analysis and discuss how this enhances the content for the reader.

Mothers Dig the Den to Give Birth

As the time approaches for the female wolf to give birth, she removes herself from the pack to prepare for a time of isolation from the rest of the pack. At this time, she begins to search for a safe and hidden location for her den. She burrows into a hillside or the lair of a more defenseless animal, digging with her front paws and shoveling the dirt behind her until all that is visible is the tip of her tail. Once inside, she angles her tunnel to provide a more secure and easily defendable home for her newborns. She remains in the den while her mate and younger members of the pack search for food and protect the place the pups will soon call home.

3. Once students have developed an understanding of analysis for support, instruct them to select a topic based on classroom research or content coverage and follow the analytic procedure modeled in Activities 1 and 2.

UNDERSTANDING APPLICATIONS IN WRITING

1. Share the following reading selection by Lance Armstrong, which analyzes the sport of cycling, with students and identify the analysis support. Although the selection is an analysis of the sport of cycling for the purpose of this activity, only address the analysis of the facts.

There are a few things I should explain here about cycling. It's an intricate, highly politicized sport, and it's far more of a team sport than most spectators realize. It has a vocabulary all its own, with words and phrases cobbled together from different languages. It has a peculiar ethic as well. On any team, each rider has a job and is responsible for some aspect of the race. The slower riders are called "domestiques" because they do the less glamorous work of protecting their team leader through the various perils of a stage race—a race that takes place over a number of days. The team leader is the principal cyclist, the rider the most capable of sprinting to a finish with 150 miles in his legs. While I started as a domestique, I was gradually groomed for the role of a team leader.

(Lance Armstrong, 2000, p. 88)

Using the definition for analysis at the beginning of this chapter, refer to the passage above to point out to students the final sentence as an example of reflective analysis.

2. Use the following questions to demonstrate how effective analysis answers questions the writer anticipates readers may have. This proactive evaluation and analysis of an intended audience reduces the opportunity for lapses in idea development to occur.

- ◆ Why do spectators not consider cycling to be a team sport? (Since there is no official "playing field," spectators may view each cyclist as an individual removed from the others on the team. In many cases, team members are not positioned in close proximity to each other during a race.)
- ◆ Why is the role of domestique important even though it is less glamorous than being a team leader? (This hierarchy of riders is similar to the bees in a hive. It is the lowest class "workers" who take care of the needs of the queen while allowing her to preserve her strength for the critical task she is to perform. In a stage race, the domestique protects the team leader for the final sprint to the finish.)
- ◆ How is the work ethic of a cyclist different from that of other athletes? (Each rider is responsible for a particular job and some aspect of the race. All riders do not receive the same level of recognition for their "work," but each must fulfill his or her task with the same level of dedication.)
- ◆ What is the significance of the phrase "the rider the most capable of sprinting to a finish with 150 miles in his legs"? (To explain the role of team leader and its significance to the success of the team, the writer describes the requirements of the leader's ability: to sprint—ride at top speed—for the final leg of the race after having ridden 150 miles.)
- ◆ How is the vocabulary specific to cycling? (Words that relate to the various aspects and requirements of the sport have been "cobbled together from different languages," probably because the sport itself is international and had its origins in Europe.)
- ◆ What does Lance Armstrong understand now about his role as a domestique that he perhaps did not recognize early in his cycling career? (He now perceives the gradual grooming of his cycling skills to match the skills required of a successful team leader.)

3. Select a short passage for the whole class to read. In small groups, students will examine and identify the ideas developed through analysis as modeled in

Activity 1 (p.112) and reflective analysis (if included). Share student responses in a group for peer or teacher input and redirection if needed. Following this feedback, students will design questions from the whole class text that would provoke a reader to analyze the information and reflect on the insight provided as modeled in Activity 2. Analysis questions should not call for *yes* or *no* responses or require only a "knowledge" response.

4. Instruct students to exchange the small group questions generated in Activity 3 with other groups in the class. Each group will then answer the questions as a means of analyzing the text. Teacher-directed discussion will ensure that students have begun to recognize how writers use analysis (including reflective analysis) as a way to provoke audience reflection and insight. Consideration of the various ways writers use analysis, including reflective analysis, in all types of writing should be addressed in the classroom on a regular basis to support content area reading material and English and language arts reading instruction.

APPLICATIONS TO WRITING

1. As a group, generate a list of possible writing topics applicable to the content being taught (or refer to any previously prepared list in a learning log or writer's notebook). After selecting a topic, each student will determine a focused purpose to address a topic. (Why might someone want or need to know about this topic?) Once a focused purpose has been established, students will determine an idea that supports their purpose and generate a set of questions that the reader might ask about the idea.

The teacher should examine and respond to each student's questions so that the student will expand the set of questions, add to the depth and complexity of the questions, and refocus the questions to more directly support the idea. Students will then provide information to answer the questions. These answers will serve as prewriting for developing ideas through analysis.

2. Students will develop their ideas, in draft form, using the analysis (answers to questions). In most cases, this draft will contain more than one paragraph. In small groups of like topics, students will exchange drafts of the ideas they have developed and answer the following questions:

- What questions has the writer answered for you?
- What are the commonalities you see in the questions this writer has answered in the writing and those answered in your own draft?
- What other questions need to be answered? Why?
- What, if any, gaps in logic are evident?

3. Students require teacher feedback regarding the effectiveness of their idea development and analysis. Provide adequate time for students to return to their working folders to reexamine previously drafted pieces, looking for places where

analysis support would add depth and promote further understanding and reflection for the audience. The writing segments produced during whole class, small group, and individual activities would be effective writing-to-learn samples for students to place in a learning log, writer's notebook, or working folder. Some students may want to develop an entire piece of writing around one of the generated ideas, whereas others may wish to use this technique for idea development in future writing. Some may choose to do nothing further with the writing generated from these activities.

ASSESSING THE EFFECTIVE USE OF ANALYSIS

As teachers or peers assess the application of analysis thinking to expand support in writing, the following criteria should be addressed.

Successful analysis will:

- ❏ Support the writer's purpose and the main idea
- ❏ Engage and involve the reader through logical, accurate, and reflective thought-provoking connections
- ❏ Interpret information through specifics related to a more general idea
- ❏ Show the relationships of the parts to one another and to the whole
- ❏ Relate developed information or ideas to other ideas, content, and personal connections
- ❏ Allow the reader to examine information or experiences more explicitly
- ❏ Establish and develop general or specific cause-and-effect or compare-and-contrast relationships
- ❏ Provide an expansion of the facts and information in the writing

EXAMPLES OF ANALYSIS TO BE USED AS CLASSROOM MODELS

Students will benefit from recognizing and examining analysis as it appears in different forms of writing. The following examples are included to provide additional classroom models. To ensure that students have internalized the concept and will make successful application in their own writing, they must be afforded many opportunities to locate and consider the effectiveness of analysis used for support. This need not be an added burden for the teacher, but rather should be an integral part of reading instruction that encourages students to think critically about their reading as well as their writing. The analysis in each of the following samples is denoted by italics.

Emily loves to be on horseback. She enjoys using something other than her wheelchair to get around. *In the saddle, Emily sits at the same level as all other riders. She's not down in her chair while everyone else is standing. In exchange for friendship, care, and a pat on the nose, Minky gives Emily a sense of freedom she can't find anywhere else.*

("Gentle Friends," 2000, p. 9)

The analysis in the example above does the following:

♦ Supports the writer's purpose and main idea
♦ Shows the relationships of the parts to one another and to the whole
♦ Interprets information through specifics related to the general idea
♦ Allows the reader to examine the experience more explicitly
♦ Establishes and develops a specific compare-and-contrast relationship
♦ Provides an expansion of the information in the writing

To recover the woodpecker, the forest service has created a buffer around this colony. *It allows "selective" harvesting of trees in a manner that does not disturb wildlife and maintains the integrity of the forest.* The forest service also regularly burns the *understory to mimic the lightning-sparked wildfires that were once part of this ecosystem. Summer burning helps regenerate wildflowers and herbs, and the open space and new ground cover attract white-tailed deer, wild turkey, and quail.*

(Greer, 1995, p. 36)

The analysis in the example above does the following:

♦ Supports the writer's purpose and the main idea
♦ Engages and involves the reader through logical, accurate, and reflective thought-provoking connections
♦ Interprets information through specifics related to a general idea
♦ Relates developed information or ideas to other content and ideas
♦ Allows the reader to examine information more explicitly
♦ Establishes and develops general and specific cause-and-effect relationships
♦ Provides an expansion of the facts and information in the writing

Fusaichi Pegasus won the Kentucky Derby and was hailed a budding superstar. Red Bullet upset him two weeks later in the Preakness, *but it was uncertain whether the result was due to Red Bullet's superiority or Fusaichi Pegasus' inability to handle the wet Pimlico track.*

(Beyer, 2000, p. C1)

The analysis in the example above does the following:

♦ Supports the writer's purpose and the main idea

- Interprets information through specifics related to a general idea
- Allows the reader to examine information more explicitly
- Establishes and develops specific compare-and-contrast relationships
- Provides an expansion of the facts in the writing

Tigers live mostly in jungles, *but they can adapt to other environments.* Tigers are found mostly in Asia, *but they can also live anywhere from freezing Antarctica to sweltering jungles.* Tigers eat up to about 100 large animals of different species per year. *This is a problem when people start to move in on tigers' territory and begin to affect the food chain. The things that tigers eat begin to die out. Then tigers don't get enough food, and they begin to die out.*

(4th-Grade Student)

The analysis in the example above does the following:

- Supports the writer's purpose and the main idea
- Engages and involves the reader through logical, accurate, and thought-provoking connections
- Interprets information through specifics related to a general idea
- Shows the relationships of the parts to one another and to the whole
- Relates developed information or ideas to other content and ideas
- Allows the reader to examine information more explicitly
- Establishes and develops general or specific cause-and-effect relationships
- Provides an expansion of the facts and information in the writing

The teachers would have twice the usual amount of instructional time. *They could use the additional time to explain things that the students do not understand. This would make the students understand the lesson better. More time in the classroom would mean more time for guided practice. New assignments could be completed with a teacher present in case students had problems. The less homework students have, the more time there would be for other activities after school. The middle school years should be a time for exploration; students need time to try new things.*

(7th-Grade Student)

The analysis in the example above does the following:

- Supports the writer's purpose and the main idea
- Engages and involves the reader through logical, accurate, and reflective thought-provoking connections
- Interprets information through specifics related to a general idea
- Shows the relationships of the parts to one another and to the whole
- Relates developed information or ideas to other ideas and personal connections

- ◆ Allows the reader to examine information more explicitly
- ◆ Establishes and develops general or specific cause-and-effect relationships
- ◆ Provides an expansion of the facts and information in the writing

> *I wish I could say I'd always been a polished writer. In fact, when I first began to plan this letter, that is precisely what I planned to do. In my arrogance—ignorance—I considered my writing the best thing to have come along since some guy named Bill Shakespeare. Luckily, however, before I wrote anything so blatantly presumptuous, blatantly arrogant, and blatantly untrue, I took a look back at some of my writing from the beginning of my high school years. And make no mistake about it; it was a slap in the face. Looking over those early writings, though, I realized just how far I'd come in four years; further, I realized just how far I'd had to come.*
>
> (12th-Grade Student)

The analysis in the example above does the following:

- ◆ Supports the writer's purpose and the main idea
- ◆ Engages and involves the reader through reflective, thought-provoking connections
- ◆ Interprets information through specifics related to a general idea
- ◆ Allows the reader to examine experiences more explicitly
- ◆ Establishes and develops specific cause-and-effect and compare-and-contrast relationships
- ◆ Provides an expansion of the facts and information in the writing

CHAPTER SUMMARY

To develop ideas through analysis, including reflective analysis, writers must become analytical readers. Therefore critical thinking about reading must be an integral part of writing instruction, and students must be provided opportunities to apply thinking strategies to their writing.

In this chapter, the teacher will lead student writers through several analysis activities that will establish a knowledge base for future application. As students become more confident in providing analysis and reflection for readers, their writing will become more sophisticated.

Teachers who look to Bloom's Taxonomy levels (Alexander, 1988, p. 219) for designing instructional practices that meet local, state, and national standards understand the importance of analysis. If students are to compete in a global environment, their analytical-thinking skills' development will be a key factor in determining their level of success. Through interconnected reading and writing instruction, astute teachers assists their students in meeting high standards.

Conclusion

The desire of educators to teach all students to communicate effectively calls for instructional solutions. Our search for best practices in writing instruction has intensified recently, due in part to the reality of national standards and pleas from the business community. As research practitioners, we have concluded that teaching the craft of writing without connecting the instruction to cognition and metacognition results in student writing devoid of depth and complexity. Sadly, problems with idea development in writing are evident throughout our daily lives, in school and out.

In this text, we have attempted to set forth an instructional solution, a sequence that begins with "deconstruction" of exemplary texts; then moves to the writer's identification of her or his own purpose and audience for a particular form or genre of writing. From that point, the instructor leads students to plan an organizational strategy for the primary ideas. We also offer possible mini-lesson sequences for teaching students the strategies effective writers use to support their primary ideas.

The type of focused, whole-text connected instruction we propose permits students to gain experiences that lead them to think critically as they compose confidently. Their reading skills and content learning expand as they become more knowledgeable about authentic texts and how to create them.

Experienced writers and student writers who have a propensity for written expression may not require the structured approach to writing outlined in this handbook. The purpose of this text, however, is not only to systematically teach writing strategies but also to develop critical-thinking applications in all communication areas—writing, speaking, and listening—and the ability to analyze written and spoken products. In our work each day, we have come to understand the importance of this type of instruction, applied in total school programs, building grade by grade.

For some students (and adults), control of written communication follows only after they learn, apply, and internalize effective habits such as these.

References

Alexander, J. E. (Ed.). (1988). *Teaching reading* (3rd ed.). Glenview, IL: Scott, Foresman.

Armstrong, L., with Jenkins, S. (2000, June). Tour de Lance. *Vanity Fair*, p. 88.

Betthauser, E. (1995). Super Mario: A member of the family. In Mary Meiser, *Good writing* (p. 160). Needham Heights, MA: Allyn & Bacon.

Beyer, A. (2000, June 1). Skipping Belmont helps colt, hurts sport. *The Washington Post*, p. C1.

Cliffhanger. (1994, November 4). *Science World, 51*, 18-19.

Darrach, B., & Petranek, S. (1995). A land of staggering proportions. In *The writer's craft* (pp. 116-117). Evanston, IL: McDougal Littell.

Dimmitt, B. (1997, April). Heading for home. *Reader's Digest*, p. 128.

Fox, M. (1995). *Wilfrid Gordon McDonald Partridge*. Sydney: Kane/Miller.

Gentle friends. (2000, March-April). *American Girl*, p. 9.

Greer, J. (1995, August). Handle with care. *Southern Living*, p. 36.

Kaminsky, M. (1995, March). Meet Bonnie Blair: The fastest woman on ice. *Highlights for Children, 50,* 10.

Kennedy, J. F. (1993, November 21). [Address given in San Antonio, Texas].

Kentucky Department of Education. (1991-1998). [Student writing samples from Kentucky Writing Portfolios].

Lassieur, A. (1995, March). Everyday inventions. *Highlights for Children, 50,* 28.

Rich, L., & Menzel, P. (1995, February). My little Dino. *Ranger Rick, 29,* 33.

Robinson, H., & Monroe, M. (1970) Louis Pasteur, a scientist is born. In *Open Highways* (p. 17). Glenview, IL: Scott, Foresman.

Scope English: Writing and Language Skills, Level 4. (1987). New York: Scholastic.

Shelton, J. (1994). *Handbook of technical writing.* Lincolnwood, IL: NCT Business Books.

Three leaf danger. (1994, March). *Current Health, 17,* 3.

Weiss, P. (1970) Zarmo the Great. In *Open Highways* (p. 36). Glenview, IL: Scott, Foresman.

Welty, E. (1995). *One writer's beginnings.* Cambridge, MA: Belknap.

**CORWIN
PRESS**

The Corwin Press logo—a raven striding across an open book—represents the happy union of courage and learning. We are a professional-level publisher of books and journals for K–12 educators, and we are committed to creating and providing resources that embody these qualities. Corwin's motto is "Success for All Learners."